LUTHERAN WOMEN IN ORDAINED MINISTRY 1970-1995

THIS BOOK OF ESSAYS is presented by Women of the ELCA on the occasion of the 25th anniversary of the ordination of women in the predecessor churches of the Evangelical Lutheran Church in America.

LUTHERAN WOMEN IN ORDAINED MINISTRY 1970-1995
REFLECTIONS AND PERSPECTIVES

Gloria E. Bengtson, Editor

Augsburg

Minneapolis

LUTHERAN WOMEN IN ORDAINED MINISTRY 1970-1995
Reflections and Perspectives

Cover and interior design: Heidi Waldmann, Eureka! Design

Library of Congress Cataloging-in-Publication Data

Lutheran women in ordained ministry 1970-1995 :   reflections and perspectives / Gloria E. Bengtson, editor.
     p.   cm.
     Includes bibliographic references.
     ISBN 0-8066-2823-5 (alk. paper)
     1. Women clergy—United States.   2. Lutheran Church—United States—Clergy—History—20th century.   I. Bengtson, Gloria E., 1949- .
BX0871.2.L88 1995   95-12713
262'.144173'082—dc20   CIP

The paper in this publication meets the minimum requirements of American National Standard for Information Sciences—Permanence of Paper for Printed Library Materials, ANSI Z329.48-1984.   ∞™

Manufactured in the U.S.A.   10-28235
03 02 01 00 99 98 97 96 95 10 9 8 7 6 5 4 3 2 1

CONTENTS

FOREWORD

THIS BOOK OF ESSAYS is presented by Women of the ELCA on the occasion of the twenty-fifth anniversary of the ordination of women in the predecessor churches of the Evangelical Lutheran Church in America.

The essays deal with the achievement of women's ordination, the experiences of ordained women in the past twenty-five years, and the impact of the ordination of women on the church.

We tried to put together a group of writers who would be representative, that would include those who had worked to achieve ordination for women, those who had been among the first women students in seminaries and the first in pulpits, those who work primarily in congregations, and those who serve in administrative offices and on seminary faculties. We are grateful to all of them for their contributions to this collection of essays, and we are thankful to Gloria Bengtson, the editor, for her excellent work and her commitment to this project.

Some people were unable to write because of the press of other responsibilities, while others who said they would write did not do so. We miss their contributions, but we hope that their stories are here, told by their colleagues and sisters.

The women who wrote of their experiences share stories of hope and joy and experiences of pain and sadness. Some write about the discrimination they encountered because they were women, others about the double discrimination they experienced as women of color. Some write about challenges and problems that are gender neutral.

There are, of course, many stories that are not here, of experiences that most ordained women would recognize immediately. There is the experience of standing at the door of the church, greeting members and visitors, and hearing the question: "Where is the *real* pastor today?" There is the fact that, on the average, women still wait longer for a first call than men, and may have more difficulty obtaining a second call. Many women have spoken with me about the special challenges ordained women face. Others have talked about the absence of role models, particularly in the early years. Several ordained women have told me, "I never heard a woman preach until I gave my first sermon."

We hoped, on the occasion of the twenty-fifth anniversary of women's ordination, to tell the story of how the ordination of women was achieved through the words of those who were there and those who have lived it. We hoped especially to tell the story of how the women of the church worked for and supported the ordination of women. As Norma Cook Everist writes, "Women would not be pastors today except for the commitment and support of lay women. . . . These women of faith believed call should be discerned on gifts, not gender, and changed the church."

Stephanie Frey supports this with her statement that "the long history of [women's] skillful lay leadership within the church had paved the way for those of us being called to take a new direction and pursue ordination. . . . It was among these [lay]women that my own sense of call to ordained ministry was confirmed. . . ."

How did the ordination of women change the church? It gave the church an opportunity to utilize more fully the talents of more than half its members. It brought a difference in outlook, a new perspective, into the pulpit, into the pastor's office, and into the whole church. As Karen Bloomquist writes, "We did not fit into either the preconceived male image of a pastor or into the ready-made clergy shirts." To paraphrase Susan Thompson's remark about Barbara Andrews, women pastors walked through the door and changed the church forever.

In celebrating the twenty-fifth anniversary of the ordination of women, we recognize that there are still miles to go to achieve full partnership for women in the church. As of this writing, two of the sixty-five synod bishops are women and there are no woman presidents of the ELCA's twenty-nine colleges or eight seminaries. Margaret Wold's question, "Are there any women. . . ?" is still relevant.

Charlotte E. Fiechter
Executive Director
Women of the ELCA

PREFACE

I AM OPEN to change but I also resist it.

The year of my ordination—1958—was the year the Church of Sweden began to debate the ordination of women. Because of my close ties with that church, I was very interested in the discussion. But if asked for my personal opinion, I would have expressed grave reservations. "It's all right for the Swedes to ordain women. But it will never work in America," I thought.

Over the next twelve years, two of our predecessor church bodies studied the issue of ordination of women. I did my homework. By 1970, when my church—the Lutheran Church in America—decided to ordain women, I was intellectually and theologically ready for it. But not emotionally.

I recall vividly the first time I saw a woman dressed in clerical garb. It was at a convention of the church in the summer of 1971. She was coming down a flight of stairs in a large hotel in Dallas. My head had done its work. But my heart was saying, "No, I'm not ready for this."

Over the next several years, my head and heart came together. I began to know several women pastors. I acknowledged my sexism. I saw the gifts they brought to the church through their ordination.

Then came an unexpected turn of events that drew me into the middle of the issue. In 1976, I was elected president of a synod and found myself directly responsible for finding places for ministry for pastors, including women. There were more than five hundred clergy on the roster, but only one woman. Over the next decade I helped open the door to ministry for sixty women. And little could I have known that my own wife would become an ordained minister of the church.

Like others who have been on this journey and seen the change, the temptation might be to think that the work is done. The door is open. Women are welcome. We need them.

But that would be naive. Yes, the door is open. But once women come through the door, they soon find that there continues to be resistance to change. In too many places, the "glass ceiling" is still firmly in place. There are congregations and other places of ministry in the Evangelical Lutheran Church in America (ELCA) that are resistant to the idea of having an ordained woman in a place of leadership. By this time, there are many women who are more than well qualified to be the senior pastor of a large congregation, or a professor of theology, or the president of one of our colleges or seminaries, or a bishop. We have had a breakthrough here and there. But in subtle and not so subtle ways women are still passed over in too many places.

For this reason, I welcome this collection of essays from those who have walked this road with me for the past twenty-five years. We may take pride in having come so far in this quarter century. We may look with impatience on churches that still do not ordain women. But we must recognize that we have come only a short distance. We have taken only the first steps. We have far to go before we can say that this church accepts women as equal partners with men in the ordained ministry of this church.

Herbert W. Chilstrom
Bishop
Evangelical Lutheran Church in America

ACKNOWLEDGMENTS

As ANYONE WHO HAS every compiled a collection of essays will tell you, it's a team effort. Each and every person recognized here has ably and generously assisted at varying stages of this project.

To all of the contributors who have shared their stories with us, thank you.

To Women of the ELCA for sponsoring this book of essays and to its executive director Charlotte Fiechter who originated the idea for the book, enabled its development, and brought a keen mind to the finished product, a special word of thanks.

I am grateful to Connie Beck, Karen Bloomquist, Gracia Grindal, Eleanor Hunsberger, DeAne Lagerquist, and Doris Pagelkopf who graciously sent in comments on material as the work progressed. And to Ann Harrington, friend and former co-worker, whose editorial competence supported the preparation of this manuscript.

In addition I offer a personal word of gratitude to Roger Gomoll, my partner in all things in this life, who taught me how to use my new computer and who offered words of support and encouragement as I ventured into the realm of self-employment.

To my parents, Alma and Arthur Bengtson, who supported me in every choice I ever made and from whom I received the gifts of life and faith, a word of thanks.

Finally, I offer thanks to the whole team at Augsburg Fortress who also helped bring this book into existence.

Gloria E. Bengtson
Editor

WE SEIZED THE SPIRIT'S MOMENT
Margaret Barth Wold

"EXCUSE ME, DR. SCHIOTZ, but are there any women on this committee?"

My question seemed an affront to the polished dignity of the conference room next to the president's office on the fourth floor of the building that housed the American Lutheran Church (ALC) offices. I had interrupted the deliberate flow of well-chosen phrases in President Frederick Schiotz's annual report to the Executive Board of American Lutheran Church Women (ALCW) for 1969. I suddenly became acutely aware that all eyes were now turned in my direction.

Briefly, I thought back to my election to the ALCW board at its Triennial Convention held in Portland, Oregon, three years earlier. I must confess that, as a pastor's wife, I had been more involved with organizing and directing Lutheran preschools and day care centers than with the women's organization. But, after my election, I had a growing sense that the women of the Lutheran church had been given a moment in God's time to effect some change in what many of us had come to believe was an unscriptural policy of the church with regard to the ordination of women.

At this first meeting of that board, I felt myself to be part of a group of women unique to their time in church history. Under the leadership of president Mildred LeRud from California and executive director Arna Njaa, both long-time advocates for full partnership for women in the church, there was a growing sense among board members that this was a historic moment in the church.

DISCRIMINATION AND RESTRICTIONS

As women in the church, many of us had become sensitive to discrimination. On the congregational level, we had been assigned to tasks that were deemed "appropriately feminine": serving dinners, quilting, taking charge of the nursery, teaching Sunday school classes, and singing in the choir. In some congregations women were still not allowed to hold office or even to speak or vote at congregational meetings. In fact, in one district of the ALC, women were not permitted to serve as delegates at district conventions until 1966. No one disciplined such congregations.

Some of us had experienced vocational restrictions. As a student of Greek and Bible at Luther College in Decorah, Iowa, I had had a powerful sense of call to become a teacher of biblical studies at one of our church colleges. At the time of my graduation I was told that women were restricted from teaching the Bible at Lutheran schools because of a biblical injunction in one of the epistles that says no woman is permitted to teach or have authority over men. I questioned the advisor who informed me of this practice, especially since I was being graduated *summa cum laude*, while male classmates of mine who had struggled through Greek and religion classes were being accepted at seminaries without any restriction. If I could do the work, why should my gender make any difference, I wondered?

Later, when I applied to the Board of Foreign Missions of the Norwegian Lutheran Church in America for work overseas, I was accepted to be a Bible teacher in China. At that time I puzzled over the fact that my Letter of Call contained no restriction against my teaching Scripture to Chinese men.

As I looked at the women seated around the conference table in Minneapolis back in 1969, I thought of the many abilities represented in the group. Each was creative, dedicated, hardworking, and capable. I knew that any one of these women could have served as a pastor had she wanted to do so and had she been given the opportunity.

I knew, of course, that not all of the ALCW staff or board members felt that changes in current policies were needed or even desired for women in the church. In fact, the body language of some of those around the table expressed some irritation at my question. As a mother of five children, I could agree with them that caring for one's children and being a homemaker was a very important vocation in itself. The ALCW's concern for women as caregivers was evidenced by the many articles about mothers and young children that appeared in *Scope*, the organization's monthly magazine.

However, we had not yet begun to address the problems facing a growing number of single mothers, or the concerns of unmarried or divorced women. Dual career marriages, with or without children, were overlooked. Noting that our membership was becoming older every year, we tended to blame younger church women for not attending ALCW meetings rather than admitting that the cause might be our own lack of programming relevant to their needs.

Since ordained men controlled church budgets and allocated program funds, many issues that were becoming vital to women both inside and outside of the church were just not being addressed.

Battered women, incest victims, female alcoholics, and discrimination in the workplace were mentioned rarely, if at all. In fact, sexual matters were largely ignored in our program resources.

For that reason, when Schiotz mentioned in his report that he had just appointed an *ad hoc* committee to study the ordination of women and to make a recommendation for or against that practice to the ALC Church Council at its meeting in June 1970, I felt a powerful conviction that this was the Spirit's moment for Lutheran women in the United States. My question was spontaneous.

"Dr. Schiotz, are there any women on this committee?"

The question hung in the air of the conference room, partly challenge, partly prayer, demanding an answer.

After a brief moment of silence, Schiotz replied, "No, and of course, there should be."

Then he asked, "Mrs. LeRud, will you appoint two women to serve on the committee?"

LeRud wasted no time. She immediately told Schiotz that Evelyn Streng, a geology professor from Texas Lutheran College in Seguin, Texas, and I would be the ALCW's representatives on his newly appointed committee.[1]

Thus, two lay women (and weren't we all lay women at that time?) joined the clergymen on the committee. With some fear and trembling because of the great weight of responsibility we both felt, but with much prayer that this might be a kairos moment for Lutheran women in the United States, we went to our first meeting.

Dr. Bruno Schlachtenhaufen, president of the Iowa District of the ALC, was chairman and Dr. William Larsen, former president of the United Evangelical Lutheran Church (UELC), was the staff person assigned to work with the committee.[2] At that time Larsen was the executive director of the Division for Theological Education of the ALC. Many years later, Schlachtenhaufen told me that up until the final meeting he had expected the committee to recommend that a study of ministry be made by the church before it made a decision on the ordination of women.

Streng and I had no mutually agreed-upon strategy in going into the meetings. We wanted to keep our minds open and to do a faithful job of reading all of the materials and weighing all the issues. Since neither one of us had had any previous contacts with the other committee members, we had no idea how any of them felt about ordination or about women. It didn't take long for the two of us to realize, however, that these men had no intention of recommending that women be permitted to join the clergy roster.

The materials on which our deliberations were based consisted mainly of studies prepared by three theologians, one man from each of the major Lutheran synods (Lutheran Church in America, American Lutheran Church, and The Lutheran Church–Missouri Synod). The Lutheran Council in the USA (LCUSA), had asked these men to make an exhaustive study of all the reasons—biblical, ecclesiastical, sociological, emotional, psychological, physiological, and so on—that were for or against the ordination of women.

We met, studied, and met again, and Streng and I were sure that the committee was going to vote against ordaining women.

Our study of the LCUSA documents and the other recommended readings had only served to strengthen our conviction that the church, by its denial of ordination to women, was in grave error and was acting contrary both to the intent of the gospel and to the practices of the earliest Christian communities.

We requested and were each given permission to address the committee. In 1969, many Lutheran lay women were searching the Scriptures for all the evidence we could find of our calling as disciples of Jesus Christ. We were reclaiming our identity as persons made in the image of God (Genesis 1:27), affirming our liberation by Jesus from patriarchal proscriptions imposed on our God-given physiological processes (Mark 5:25-34; see Leviticus 15:19-30), and acting on our conviction that Jesus had given his blessing to women as bearers of the Word of God (Luke 11:27-28).

Our quest was a lonely one. Women who are considered major theologians now were little known in the 1960s. Mary Daly's landmark work, *The Church and the Second Sex*, was published (by Harper & Row) in 1968. I had found her book, along with Krister Stendahl's *The Bible and the Role of Women* (Fortress Press, 1966), helpful reading. But, oddly enough, it was a Missouri Synod pastor's study of the relevant scriptures that had motivated my own journey most significantly. The book by Russell C. Prohl was published in 1957 (Eerdman's, Grand Rapids, Mich.) and entitled *Women in the Church*.

Streng was the first to address the committee. When she spoke, I could hear the strong emotion behind her words, and I felt that same emotion trembling in my own voice when I spoke. There was no way we could hide the pain of so many years of our perceived devaluation by God and our rejection as whole persons by the church we loved and served.

Apparently our presentations were effective. When Larsen, at our final meeting, came with a strong and positive resolution that the ALC Church Council recommend the ordination of women to the General Convention that fall, it was accepted unanimously.

When members of the ALCW Executive Board received the report on the resolution to go before the ALC Church Council, they were so confident that both the council and the convention would support the recommendation that a victory celebration was planned to replace the routine oral report of the ALCW president, a report that was included on the agenda of every biennial convention of the church.

Our board report was scheduled immediately before the convention was to vote on the ordination resolution. But, instead of the ALCW president standing up on the platform alone, all of us—board members and staff—marched in to the convention hall to the strains of "When the Saints Go Marching In." Clapping and singing along with the recorded voice of Nat King Cole, we brought the mostly male delegation to their feet.

The vote that followed was more than enough to carry the motion.[3]

It was indeed the Spirit's moment for women in the American Lutheran Church.

Notes

1. Gracia Grindal, "How Lutheran Women Got to Be Ordained," *Lutheran Women in Ordained Ministry 1970-1995: Reflections and Perspectives* (Minneapolis: Augsburg Books, 1995), pp. 33-44.
2. Other committee members were Dr. E. Clifford Nelson and the Rev. John Thoreson.
3. The resolution was adopted by the October 1970 biennial convention of the ALC in San Antonio, 560 to 414, with one abstention.

GOD AT WORK AMONG US
Dorothy J. Marple

THE SPIRIT MOVES where it will. The inflaming and renewing spirit worked for women's ordination throughout the history of Lutheran Church in America's Lutheran Church Women (LCW) and its predecessor groups. But the catalytic experience that gave the final push to women's ordination was a workshop on racism. These three streams—the work of the Holy Spirit, the legacy of predecessor women's auxiliaries, and the workshop on racism—paved the way for the statement adopted by the LCW Board of Directors in support of women's ordination. The statement laid some of the groundwork for the 1970 Lutheran Church in America (LCA) convention action that made the ordination of women possible. It gave public notice that Lutheran women intended to unite and open doors to ordained ministry long closed to them in the church.

BUILDING ON A LEGACY
For more than a century women's organizations were identified as promoters and financial supporters of the church's mission task at home and throughout the world. Even though in the early years the dictates of men circumscribed their purpose and existence, these organizations were major vehicles for women's involvement and leadership in the church.

Integral to their witness and service in local congregations and in the "uttermost parts of the world" was an emphasis on the nurture of women and their relationship to the triune God through prayer, daily offerings, and educational activities. Leadership training affirmed God-given gifts and prepared women to use these gifts in service to others. The recruitment of women for overseas missionary service accompanied by scholarship and salary support, cracked open the door for a role in the church beyond that of volunteer. National church women's organizations learned to adapt to change as church mergers took place over the years and in so doing began to set the stage for the transformation of the role of women in the church.

Building on this legacy, LCW, from its beginning in 1962, explored ways to understand its mission within North America and worldwide. The escalation of the war in Vietnam and the racial unrest and upheaval in urban centers in the United States made it a tense and tumultuous time. Rapid social change was pervasive. The roles of women and men were changing dramatically in society. Board and staff tracked social trends and probed implications for women striving to live as Christians. Social concerns of the 1990s—hunger, illiteracy, women and children in poverty, ecology, criminal justice, welfare reform—were beginning to emerge in the 1960s as challenges to our engagement in mission.

Two years before the 1970 LCA action to ordain women, the 1968 LCW Triennial Convention adopted "New Ways for New Days," three-year objectives that affirmed the "necessity of examining and responding to diverse and complex changes in the world in which we live." Specific goals called for strategies to work for justice through legislation and social planning, in joining with others to gain basic human rights for all people, in making a commitment "to the development and use of unique personal resources in responsible concern for self and others."

Advocacy for deeper self-understanding and responsibility as Christian women was implicit in these objectives and goals. Educational resources prepared by LCW sharpened understanding of current social issues and trends and challenged women to be bearers of love and justice in family, church, and community life. Bible studies introduced new insights into being the people of God and stressed applying what was learned to life situations. *Lutheran Women*, the official periodical, attuned women to changing emphases in the church's mission, to new roles of women and areas for serving and seeking justice, and to the importance of advocacy for Christian social action. Leadership training experiences, designed to include membership development, reflected the calling of women to be whole persons in Christ and equipped them to assume leadership roles. In short, the hard shell of custom and tradition that circumscribed roles of women in the church was being cracked.

The president of LCW, Doris H. Spong, an energetic and committed churchwoman, was a lifelong supporter and advocate for the full participation of women in the church. She brought a compelling, far-reaching vision for the education and training of women for leadership in church and society, and for expanding the opportunities for the service of women in all expressions of the church in North America and globally through the Lutheran World Federation and the World Council of Churches. In later years she disclosed her deep frustration with church leaders who would not open doors through changes in policy and practices to expand the role of women in the church. Spong used every opportunity to help women affirm themselves, to value their gifts as from God and use them with abandon. She never hesitated to challenge the president of the church and other leaders when women were not given their due representation in church delegations or recognized for their contributions in leadership and service in the church.

A CATALYTIC EXPERIENCE

Advocacy for women's full participation in all areas of the church's life took a new turn as the result of a catalytic experience in an intense twenty-four-hour encounter with a team of black American community leaders and LCA staff. This encounter was a part of the churchwide Priority Program for Justice and Social Change aimed to expose the sin of white racism. Board members and LCW staff peeled back layers of accumulated and entrenched attitudes, thoughts, and behavioral actions that enslave others. Their own participation as white Americans in discrimination and injustice became recognizable as they grappled with the reality that racism was their problem and they needed to change. They came face to face with their own involvement in structures and practices that denied the equality of all people before God.

The effects of the encounter experience were both penetrating and empowering. The quiet but articulate and powerful story of one of the leaders who spoke of what it meant to be a black American laid bare oppressive structures that not only prevented persons from exploring their full capacities but also distorted personal identity and self-image. Dealing with negative and false images of black Americans frequently projected by white persons opened up the discussion of the image of women and their subordination in the church. It was a short step to a more profound understanding of the structures within the church that stunted the personal growth of women and limited the possibilities for creative expansion of talents and abilities for service.

In the hours that elapsed between the close of the encounter experience and the plenary meeting of the LCW board when the statement supporting the ordination of women was adopted, board members and staff talked together in twos and threes, some into the night. They wrestled with what equality before God and freedom in Christ meant—not only in race relations, but also in relationships between husbands and wives, in work settings, and in service and leadership opportunities within the church. A small committee, appointed by the president, drafted a resolution in support of women's ordination. "It was God at work that night among us," recalled Spong. "Not only were we thinking about our own racist feelings and actions, but also how women needed freedom to use their God-given gifts in service to others in every part of the church's life."

Spong and other board members were aware of the continuing work of the Commission on the Comprehensive Study of the Doctrine of Ministry that the LCA convention authorized in 1964. Despite the conclusion of the commission report to the 1968 LCA convention stating there were no biblical or theological reasons for denying ordination of women, it made no recommendation to ordain women lest such an act would threaten ecumenical fellowship. However, the LCW board learned that the 1970 commission report stated that "both men and women are eligible for call and ordination" and would be accompanied by a recommendation to make this position a reality. This came as good news. The time was right, even past time according to some board members, for women to be ordained. The question no longer was whether women should be ordained. It was a matter of rights and justice for women. Now was the time for women to do something for women, to provide support that would allow them to make vocational choices freely according to their aspirations and gifts. Church tradition, customs, and structures that denied equal opportunity for women were barriers to be penetrated. Freedom in Christ meant freedom for all regardless of race or gender.

After hearing a proposed statement supporting women's ordination newly drafted by a committee appointed by the LCW president, the board decision came quickly and decisively. The unanimous action put the LCW board on record as advocating the ordination of women and calling the entire church to take next steps "creatively and vigorously" in implementation.

The board's action was comprehensive. It called on seminaries to publicize that they welcomed women students, to create a climate of acceptance, to provide adequate personal counseling for them, and to call women to their faculties and encourage women to pursue advanced study. The action asked LCA synodical presidents actively to seek calls for women candidates and encourage congregations to call women pastors. The LCW board urged churchwide and synodical boards, commissions, and committees to provide for the full participation of ordained women as elected representatives or professional staff in decision-making, planning, and administrative responsibilities.

ADVOCACY AT LCA CONVENTION

The full text of the comprehensive statement was widely distributed to all seminary presidents, synodical presidents, and board and agency executives. Minimal and generally lukewarm response intensified the need for strong advocacy. LCW board members attending the 1970 LCA convention as delegates from their respective synods prepared to speak on the convention floor in support of the necessary constitutional and bylaw changes that would enable the ordination of women. Caucus meetings of women delegates and visitors provided mutual encouragement and strengthened the resolve to stand together for justice for women. Women seminarians and women with previous theological education who had been denied the possibility of being ordained brought energy and passion for an affirmative convention action. When the question of women's ordination came before the convention, it took less than an hour for a decision to be made, with a resounding "yes" voice vote. Board members at the convention planned strategy to lay before the church the next steps to translate this ground-breaking action into reality. The Reverend Frederick K. Wentz, president of Hamma Theological School, had received the LCW board statement and had made a supportive response. Spong talked with him about giving public support to the concerns addressed in the LCW statement. Wentz agreed and presented in slightly modified form the content of the statement. The motion was quickly adopted and became a reference point for action strategies in support of ordained women.

FOLLOW-UP TO CONVENTION ACTION

Lutheran Church Women did not view the LCA convention decision to ordain women as the time to step aside and leave the implementation to others. Rather, the organization made intentional decisions to continue its role as supporter and advocate over the long term. These decisions permeated the program of the organization during the seventies and eighties. A long-time provider of scholarships for women in higher education, LCW immediately recognized the need for financial assistance for theological students from minority groups and women in continuing theological education. It earmarked a specific portion of its gift to the LCA for such assistance.

When possibilities for appointing women to seminary faculties were reported to be limited due to lack of a sufficient number of candidates with the necessary academic credentials, the LCW board designated one-half of the Centennial Observance Offering in 1981 for women preparing for church leadership, providing grants to women doing graduate work in the theological disciplines. The challenge of helping to create a climate of acceptance of women pastors in congregations was a continuing concern. Deliberate efforts were made to give all LCW members chance to recognize and appreciate the gifts of ordained women. These women were engaged as writers for Bible studies, educational resources, and magazine stories. *Lutheran Women* consistently featured articles about the ministry of both ordained and lay women. Lutheran Church Women synodical unit leaders were alerted to the contribution they could make by inviting women pastors as preachers, Bible study leaders, and major presenters at conventions and other gatherings. To build bridges of friendship and mutual support, LCW gave women seminarians scholarships to attend triennial conventions. Systemic and organizational issues and theological considerations related to the participation of women in the life and work of the church were pursued through participation in the LCA Consulting Committee on Women in Church and Society. Regular reports to the LCW Board of Directors reinforced the need to be persistent and engaged in providing support and initiating change in attitudes and actions.

Twenty-five years is a relatively short period of history but significant in reflecting on the ordination of women. The action to ordain women was an important sign of accountability to the gospel. It was a new beginning. No longer could the ministry of Word and sacrament be assumed to be a male province or prerogative. All women benefited because ultimately the struggle was not only for rights and equal opportunity for ministry according to talents and ability, but for recognition of all women as persons of worth. The struggle persists and the Spirit continues to move where it will. Lutheran Church Women was privileged to be an advocate and continuing supporter of women's ordination.

NOW IS THE KAIROS— THE RIGHT TIME
Mary Todd

WHEN, IN 1969, representatives of the three major Lutheran church bodies came together in Dubuque, Iowa, to share the findings of their joint study on the ordination of women, the event passed without most members of The Lutheran Church–Missouri Synod (LCMS) knowing about it.

There were far more pressing matters for the synod, whose Denver convention in 1969 had sent mixed messages to its own membership and to other Lutherans as well. The church elected a new and more conservative president, Jacob A. O. Preus, while approving both woman suffrage, the right of women to vote in congregational meetings (after thirty years of study), and fellowship with the American Lutheran Church (ALC). So, at the Dubuque consultation only a few months later, when LCMS representatives agreed to disagree with the conclusions of the study (which found no scriptural basis either for ordination or forbidding it), the ordination of women became a closed question. That issue remains as one of the wedges between the Missouri Synod and the Evangelical Lutheran Church in America (ELCA) these twenty-five years later.

The situation in the Missouri Synod only worsened after 1969. Conservatives who argued for biblical literalism and inerrancy disagreed with the historical-critical method being taught at Concordia Seminary, St. Louis. In 1973 moderate members who were determined to stay in their spiritual home founded Evangelical Lutherans in Mission (ELiM) as a confessing movement.

When the seminary controversy escalated and led to the establishment of Concordia Seminary in Exile (Seminex) in February 1974, the critical pieces were in place for schism in the synod. When Preus removed four district presidents from office in the spring of 1976 over the issue of ordaining Seminex graduates, a core group from ELiM separated from Missouri and incorporated as the Association of Evangelical Lutheran Churches (AELC). Now outside the reach of the Missouri Synod, the new church was asked by the still governing ELiM board to "recognize the full participation of women in the whole ministry of the church, including the pastoral office."[1]

This was not the first time the question of the ordination of women had been raised among the moderates who left the synod. In March 1976 the faculty of Seminex certified for ordination a female student, Jan Otte, who was due to graduate from the seminary in May. *Missouri in Perspective* reported her certification as the "strongest statement to date on the issue of women's service in the church."[2] Even before this dramatic development, Otte suggested there had been the expectations caught up in Seminex itself: the inclusion of women students represented a hope that women might be ordained.[3] And ELiM women had met that May to launch "a campaign to seek churchwide support for the ordination of women" and declared that "Now is the kairos—the right time—in the church and society for women to be ordained."[4]

What appears over and over again in the recollections of women and men who lived the struggle of the AELC is a sense of newness and opportunity to do things differently. Some of the desire to make changes was in reaction to the church body they had left. They would be defined by who they were not, and they were no longer Missouri Synod. But reaction against the church they had left is not in itself an adequate explanation for the decision to ordain women. The Missouri Synod had almost no experience with women as equal participants in its congregations. In 1969, before the church changed its position on woman suffrage, women were allowed to attend voters' meetings in only ten percent of synod congregations and to vote in only one percent of congregations.[5]

These developments took place alongside major changes in church and society. In the early 1970s a second wave of feminism took hold among American women. The Equal Rights Amendment was proposed by Congress in 1972 after having first been introduced in 1923, though it subsequently failed to be ratified. The Equal Credit Act, Title IX and the Education Amendments to the Civil Rights Act, and no-fault divorce laws were all enacted by the mid-1970s, forever changing the possibilities available to American women. In academia, feminist scholarship began to introduce gender as a category of analysis, and emerging feminist theology quickly became a legitimate focus of study regarding the place of women in church and society.

Lutheran women, like their sisters in other traditions, took various stances on the challenges offered by feminism. A significant part of the AELC story is the contribution of the Lutheran Women's Caucus, organized primarily by Missouri Synod women in Chicago in 1970 and dedicated to promoting the equality of women and men. Soon labeled radical by the synod, the Caucus's primary successes were in raising the consciousness of women through study. While their focus was on the "whole woman" and not on ordination, the Caucus developed resource packets it called Sistersources and provided an important alternative model for women in the church.[6]

There is significant overlap among members of the Caucus and women who came together following the founding of the AELC to create a woman's organization. Struggling to understand themselves as women in this new church and to see women as church, Women in Action for Mission (WAM) came into being in 1978. WAM was determined to be both non-hierarchical and woman-owned, "a whole new way of working," according to Sammy Mayer, who served as national coordinator of the organization.[7] The women involved were all "people who understood theology, they understood their place as disciples within the church, and they . . . were at a juncture in the church's history where they were willing to risk stepping into new territory."[8] That new territory included women in public ministry, and WAM was significant in its support of women clergy.[9]

There always has to be a pioneer in a story like this. The AELC's was Jan Otte.[10] Otte was called to both a residential crisis counseling center and the University Chapel at Berkeley. She was ordained on Reformation Sunday 1977 in San Francisco after the Pacific Regional Synod of the AELC, in its constituting convention, approved the ordination of women. The Lutheran Bay Area Women's Coalition, which had studied biblical models of women in a series of retreats led by Lutheran Council in the USA (LCUSA) staff person Joanne Chadwick, and which had urged Otte's ordination, was very much a part of the service. This coalition of women celebrated not just one woman but women in the church as a whole, because in the AELC ordination was only part of a broader movement about women's leadership, both clergy and lay. Women were interested not in another women's organization but in being leaders in the church. Some wanted to be ordained and some didn't. The diversity and inclusiveness so fundamental to the AELC's organizing principles allowed both.[11]

What remains remarkable about the ordination of women in the AELC is the ease with which it happened. It had not been a prevailing issue in the synodical controversy that led to the formation of the AELC, though there were women students at the seminary at the time of the exile. The topic was not the subject of great debate or study once proposed to the leaders of the new church body. The decision was reached, synod by synod, at the initiative of people at the grassroots of the AELC who saw in the denial of women's ordination a stifling of the Spirit and of creative options for ministry. Congregations took time to study the question before synods took action. Some congregations supported women in ministry but couldn't afford additional pastoral salaries, yet offered women calls for a dollar a year to enable them to serve as clergy.

Critics at the time said it shouldn't have happened so quickly, and one might concur that, seen in relation to the pain of schism, the issue of women's ordination was too important to be just swept in with the other changes that were taking place. There was admittedly little thought about what this step would mean for women or for congregations. But the ordination of women was a crucial piece in the identity and mission of the AELC. It helped define who they were not, while providing a link to the other Lutherans they eventually hoped to join, and did.

Notes

1. *Missouri in Perspective*, July 19, 1976, p. 7.

2. *Missouri in Perspective*, March 15, 1976, pp. 3, 7.

3. Jan Otte, interview with author, tape recording, November 3, 1994. On hope, see Marie Schroeder, "Issues: Trouble Enough? Women's Ordination," *Missouri in Perspective*, August 2, 1976, p. 5.

4. *Missouri in Perspective*, May 24, 1976, p. 7.

5. Margaret Sittler Ermarth, *Adam's Fractured Rib: Observations on Women in the Church* (Philadelphia: Fortress Press, 1970), p. 115.

6. Gretchen Leppke, interview by author, tape recording, November 2, 1994.

7. Sammy Mayer, interview transcript, Archives of Cooperative Lutheranism ALC-AELC-LCA OHC Oral History Collection, ELCA Archives, Chicago, p. 8.

8. *Ibid.*, p. 10.

9. Leppke interview, November 2, 1994.

10. Jan Otte, "Breaking Away," *Lutheran Women in Ordained Ministry 1970-1995: Reflections and Perspectives* (Minneapolis: Augsburg Books, 1995), pp. 59-65.

11. Joanne Chadwick, interview by author, tape recording, November 12, 1994.

HOW LUTHERAN WOMEN CAME TO BE ORDAINED

Gracia Grindal

AROUND 10:00 P.M. on June 29, 1970, the Lutheran Church in America, in convention in Minneapolis, voted after a brief debate to change "man" in the bylaws that defined a minister of the church to "person." With that, Lutheran women could be ordained in this country for the first time.

This approval of women pastors in the Lutheran churches of America, now twenty-five years in the past, is a thing to be remarked. Women's ordination was not a priority of the Reformation, though it is fair to say that women could not have been ordained without such reforms as Martin Luther began some 475 years ago. How did we get here from there? And what exactly is there about women pastors that is uniquely possible because of the Reformation? And now that we are here, what barriers exist to the continued flourishing of women pastors? These questions are all before us as we consider the effects of decisions made by the American Lutheran Church (ALC) and the Lutheran Church in America (LCA) some twenty-five years ago. And since Lutherans are by confession and inclination interested in what Scripture has to say about these issues, it is in the Bible we should begin.

As the question of ordaining Lutheran women began to be asked in the 1950s in this country, many Lutheran women looked to the examples of women in the Bible as warrants for their own ordination. Women of the twentieth century, however, were not the first to have noticed that Jesus called women into ministry. From the beginning when the women of the Roman Empire became followers of the Way, they were aware that Jesus' attitude toward women was different from that of most public leaders of the time. He was a good friend of Mary and Martha, he spoke with a Samaritan woman whom every other Jewish male of his day would have shunned, and he sent Mary Magdalene, the first witness to his resurrection, to tell the good news to his disciples.

It is important to remember, however, that in Luke's Gospel, where the twelve are featured most prominently, none of the disciples is a woman. And as the second coming of the Lord seemed to be delayed and the church became more established and organized, women's roles declined, and then vanished, into the mists of history. One can see this diminishing role clearly in the New Testament where women are first admonished not to prophesy with uncovered heads, then not to be in a teaching role over a man, and then to be silent. The charismatic outbreak of the Spirit on the day of Pentecost where "in the last days both the sons and daughters shall dream dreams" (Acts 2:17) was gradually routinized into the theocratic structures of the Roman Empire, and then the structures of the medieval church, in which only men could preach or administer the sacraments. Gradually, through the medieval period, the practice of having celibate male priests performing the Mass became a theological principle that still dominates the thinking of John Paul II, the current bishop of Rome. In this thinking, the Mass was a drama in which the sacrifice of Christ was re-presented by the priest, acting as Christ and, in fact, representing him. Visually and dramatically this representation required a male presence resembling Jesus. The priest's ability to perform the sacrament depended upon his being ordained by a bishop who stood in direct succession to the twelve apostles, all of whom were male. Without ordination by such a bishop the Mass was invalid.

It is this theological understanding of the Mass, with some modifications, that stands at the heart of John Paul II's adamant refusal to consider the ordination of women. These theological reasons, not mere sexism, remain still today in the Roman Catholic church and parts of the Anglican communion, where the ordination of women priests is regarded as an abomination. The Orthodox churches also share much of this theological and historical opinion of the ordination of women.

When Luther began his reformation of the church's theology, he struck at the heart of this system by attacking the notion of the Mass as a sacrifice—a dramatic event staged to represent the Last Supper—that by its very reenactment obtained merits for the church that it could then distribute to sinners. Tetzel, the German monk who sold indulgences for the church in crude but successful ways—"as soon as a coin in the coffer rings, a soul from Purgatory springs!"—represents perfectly the medieval system as it was experienced by Luther. Nothing but faith could obtain the merit of salvation for Luther, and nothing but the free grace of God in Jesus Christ could save. As Luther began to work out the implications for Christian life that flowed from his famous *solas*—faith alone, grace alone, Word alone—the medieval structures came tumbling down. The pope and his prelates did not miss this frontal attack on their authority and responded. As they did, Luther in his multitudinous pamphlets began working out the doctrine of vocation and ministry that marked his reformation and gave women a new way to think of their roles in society.

Luther asserted that all Christians, both male and female, were called to serve their neighbor and the world. Free of constant worry about their eternal salvation, they could now turn to their vocations as Christians living in this world, with a wholesome appetite for its pleasures—marriage, family, food, drink. For Luther it was not religious to shun the physical world.

Christians were also called into ministry—the priesthood of all believers—where they were to offer the mutual consolation of the saints to their neighbors and speak God's healing word of grace and forgiveness to those who needed to hear it. This meant that men and women could read the Bible in their own language and interpret it without the necessity of a priest to tell them what it meant. Luther even stressed the fact that girls should receive an education so they could read the Bible. It was not important who spoke the reconciling word, what was important was that the Word was spoken. In Luther's theology, it was the Word that had the power to do all, not the one who spoke it. It should not be difficult to see how Luther, with this theology, broke the medieval system at its heart and unleashed a powerful social change on Europe. When knowledge and power were no longer dominated by the clergy, the energy of Protestantism broke out all over Nothern Europe. The momentum even frightened Luther, who pulled back from some of his more radical ideas when the peasants, urged on by their understanding of his reformation, began to revolt against the powers that be.

Luther's marriage to Katherine von Bora profoundly affected the place of women in Luther's society. Women with religious vocations married and began to have children. Whether it has been proven that housewifery was better for women's intellectual life than convent life is not clear, but it was a profound change in the religious understanding of the people of the time. Katherine, legend has it, was a former nun who convinced Luther to marry her. An older man at the time, Luther had spent the majority of his mature years in exclusively monastic company and was heir to centuries of misogynist literature. Yet his insights into the estate of marriage and the place of women seem remarkable by any standard.

Luther deserves credit for two developments that went a long way toward making the ordination of women possible, though this was admittedly not his first intention: (1) he smashed the theology of the Mass as a sacrifice performed by a male priest resembling Christ; (2) he taught that women could have a Christian vocation while married and without having to be in a religious order.

While there is some record of accomplished women participating in the intellectual life of the Reformation, they did not have much of a public voice. Women first appeared as public voices in the church in the great mission movement of the nineteenth century when, having heard the call of God to give witness to salvation in Jesus Christ, they left by the thousands as missionaries to far-off shores.

Lutheran women were among those women who heard this call to come and help. And they made an important contribution to the ultimate struggle to get women ordained. When they came home from the mission field, they modeled for many people what a woman preacher would be like, since they frequently addressed congregations with edifying speeches that were indistinguishable from sermons.

But the question of women pastors was not broached among Lutherans until 1938, when the Church of Norway voted to allow the ordination of women; it did not ordain one until more than twenty years later. Missionary women were occasionally accepted into seminary courses, but it was not until the late 1950s that the question of ordination was asked formally among American Lutherans.

On December 5, 1958, President Alvin Rogness of Luther Seminary informed the faculty that he planned to discuss with the district presidents of the Evangelical Lutheran Church (ELC) whether or not women should be admitted to the seminaries of the church in preparation to becoming pastors.[1] Given the approaching merger of the ALC (in 1960) and the LCA (in 1962), the question of women's ordination was, predictably, put on hold in both groups while other, more pressing, matters of organization were settled. The new Board of Education of the ALC began considering the question as women began to press for entrance into its seminaries in the mid-1960s. In 1964, Luther Seminary, for example, accepted Barbara Andrews as its first full-time female student and granted her the right to take homiletics and other pre-ordination courses. Andrews was joined by another woman that same year. However, the Board of Theological Education of the ALC did not approve of women's ordination at the time and stipulated that the women enrolled at the seminaries could study theology, but not expect to be certified for ordination.

Thus it was that Lutherans in America began to consider the question formally. The conversation began officially in the LCA in 1966, at the LCA's second convention, when a study on ministry called for a further look at the "question of ordaining women."[2] It is interesting to note that the first objections to the question came from those who were interested in its effect on the ecumenical movement, which was flourishing at that time. One LCA theologian, Phillip A. Heffner, wrote that women's ordination could be "offensive" to our ecumenical partners in the Catholic church,[3] and Franklin Clark Fry, the president of the LCA, also argued that it would offend "the great bulk of Christendom, the Roman Catholic and Orthodox churches."[4]

In that same year, 1966, the Board of Theological Education of the ALC reported that it had permitted a woman to enroll at Luther Seminary with the intention of being ordained. Both the ALC and the LCA treated the question of ordaining women seriously and began to address the question in a variety of committees and consultations. The 1968 LCA convention, stunned by the recent death of Fry, heard a report from its new ministry study committee that it had agreed there were no "biblical or theological reasons for denying ordination to women."[5] That same year the ALC convention heard a report from its Church Council to the effect that it was treating the question seriously. Both conventions, however, seem to have been more preoccupied with issues of civil rights and anti-war attitudes among the delegates.

Just one week after the ALC's 1968 convention, however, the Luther Seminary faculty, pressed by several of its women students, issued a statement on the question of women's ordination. The statement listed four common objections to the ordination of women: biblical, theological, practical, and ecumenical. The first three were a draw: none of them gave the church a clear signal as to what to do. The biblical injunctions against women speaking in church or having leadership were contradicted by ample evidence that women had had important leadership roles in the early church, in fact, Paul's admonition that women prophesy in church only with their heads covered indicated that women did speak in church. The confessions said nothing either for or against women preaching. The practical reasons of tradition and the social situation of the time gave no clear advice either. For this reason, the faculty advised that the most serious objection was ecumenical: Choosing to ordain women would further divide the Christian church. They concluded, however, "We can see no valid reason why women candidates for ordination who meet the standards normally required for admission to the ministry should not be recommended for ordination."[6]

That same autumn the Executive Committee of Lutheran Council in the USA (LCUSA) appointed a four-person subcommittee on the ordination of women that was to report in January of 1969. It concluded, in a Statement of Findings, essentially what the Luther Seminary faculty had concluded:

(a) that the biblical and theological evidence is not conclusive either for or against the ordination of women;

(b) that the sociological, psychological, and ecumenical considerations do not settle the question;

(c) that variety in practice on this question is legitimate within common Lutheran confessions;

(d) that the decision of the individual Lutheran church bodies should be made only after consultation with the other bodies and in sensitivity to the other Christian churches;

(e) that the question of the ordination of women involves the broader question of ordination itself, the office of the ministry, the ministry of the whole people of God."[7]

This statement and subsequent meetings of the subcommittee began to raise complications among The Lutheran Church–Missouri Synod (LCMS) representatives who were divided on the question, and whose recently elected president, Jacob A. O. Preus, was critical of the historical-critical method of reading the Bible implicit in the work of the subcommittee. A consultation on the question was held at Wartburg Theological Seminary on September 20-22, 1969. Three representatives from each church body were chosen to meet and thoroughly discuss the question. (The participants were: from the ALC Roy Harrisville, William Larsen, Stanley D. Schneider; from the LCA Margaret Sittler Ermarth, Martin J. Heinecken, Ralph Peterson; from the

LCMS Fred Kramer, Martin H. Scharlemann, Edward H. Schroeder; and from the Evangelical Lutheran Synod (ELS), Kenneth Ballas.) The consultation found that the most vexing argument was the one concerning "the orders of creation" that had been argued by Martin Scharlemann. According to this argument, the created orders, established by God after the fall, put women in subjection to men and meant that they could never teach or preach. This turned out to be the most sensitive point of the consultation and it recommended there be further study on the issue.

Women were also arguing the question. The American Lutheran Church Women (ALCW), at its 1966 Triennial Convention in Minneapolis voted to study the issue, and at the board's initiative ALC president Frederick Schiotz appointed Evelyn Streng and Margaret Wold to the committee of five set up by the ALC Church Council to make a recommendation to the 1970 church convention.[8] At the February 3, 1970 meeting of LCUSA, with all three church presidents in attendance, the report of the Division of Theological Studies of LCUSA was accepted. The division was then asked to prepare a report that would be made available to all pastors and congregations in the respective churches. Raymond Tiemeyer of the LCA prepared the document for distribution by May of 1970 and all three presidents distributed the report, even Preus, who sent it out with a letter criticizing what he felt to be the flippant tone of the study.

By this time three women had graduated from Luther Seminary. An ALC congregation had voted unanimously to call one of them, Dawn Proux, but she was not issued a call since the ALC Church Council would not authorize her ordination until the study process was completed. *The Lutheran* (published by the LCA) and *The Lutheran Standard* (published by the ALC), in preparation for the biennial conventions, began presenting the question, but the debate appeared not to be very fierce; it seemed to be just one among many other more pressing issues of a turbulent, revolutionary time.

At the same time Lutheran Church Women (LCW) of the LCA was urging the ordination of women.[9] Margaret Sittler Ermarth wrote the most substantial book on the question,

Adam's Fractured Rib. She argued the case from more sociological and feminist sources than theological, as did Constance Parvey and LaVonne Althouse in various journals of the church. In contrast, Margaret Wold, soon to become director of the ALCW, argued largely from Scripture. These two approaches still continue among women in the Evangelical Lutheran Church in America (ELCA), as they debate their loyalties to feminism and the Gospel. These two sides of what has now become the culture wars in American church and political life could be said to have begun developing here for many Lutheran women.

In July 1970 the LCA convention was presented with a thorough "Report of the Commission on the Comprehensive Doctrine of the Ministry" that recommended the ordination of women because "there was nothing in the exercise of the ordained ministry as a functional office that would exclude a woman because of her sex."[10] After a brief debate, the LCA convention approved the ordination of women.

The ALC convention met in October of that same year. Schiotz urged the delegates to use "sanctified common sense" in their decision since Scripture gave no clear word on the issue.[11] After a brief debate, the resolution passed, 560 to 414, with one abstention. Now women could be ordained in two of the largest Lutheran churches in America. But the other large Lutheran church, the LCMS, would question the ALC's vote as it considered pulpit and altar fellowship with the ALC.

Since the objection to the ordination of women had come from those who argued that women had to be in submission to men, according to the so-called "orders of creation" doctrine developed out of an interpretation of Adam's headship over Eve after the fall, Kent Knutson, newly-elected president of the ALC, asked the three ALC theological faculties to consider the question of headship and ministry. All three came back with a resounding critique of the interpretation of women's subordination to men.

These issues were also being fought out, to disastrous conclusions, in the Missouri Synod.[12] As the struggles between John Tietjen, president of Concordia Seminary, St. Louis, and Preus grew over how the LCMS was to interpret Scripture, the faculty and student body at Concordia Seminary continued the fight as it had begun in LCUSA. Robert Bertram, of the Concordia faculty and a member of the LCUSA subcommittee, had some years before agreed with the Statement of Findings. When the conflict boiled over many students and faculty at Concordia felt it necessary to establish Seminex, a seminary in exile. The issue of women's ordination, though not central to the conflict, was quickly settled. Women could study at Seminex and in 1976 the new Association of Evangelical Lutheran Churches (AELC), formed by those who found it impossible to continue to do ministry within the LCMS, passed a statement saying that women could be ordained. Jan Otte, a Seminex graduate was ordained to ministry in the AELC in 1977.

Thus, by 1977, all the Lutheran churches that would later join together in the ELCA had approved the ordination of women and had ordained them.

The historical data make clear how deliberately theological the churches were in their efforts to address the issue of women's ordination. The question of ordaining women was addressed among theological professors and in seminary settings. Discussions were taken seriously. The strident debate one associates with any issue that eventually came to the floor of conventions during these times is simply missing. It feels, at this distance, like a matter whose time had come, even for those who did not like it.

Later, as the presence of women clergy began to increase, the question was perhaps felt more deeply as congregations struggled to overcome their long experience of not having women pastors. The debate became more strident, perhaps, as it became more focused in local situations. So it is not surprising that it was after the ordination of women that the various churches established committees to make the place of women in the church equal to men, and it is out of this concern that the representational principles of the ELCA were established and are now defended.

Now that women have been pastors for a generation, the question would seem to have been settled, though one can hear low grumblings about how quickly the decision was made in

1970 and how little theological reflection there was to support the decision. While it is true that the vote was quickly taken, it is not true that there was little theological reflection. One can see from the lists of documents and studies that it was carefully considered and all of the objections clearly laid out.

The ecumenical question, however, still lurks in the background. If the decision of the Anglican Church to ordain women caused Pope John Paul II to declare that Rome and Canterbury were now in "impaired" communion, what does he think of our ordaining of women? Although the official ecumenical movement may well have dissolved into thin air, there will be some questions still looming before the ELCA in 1997 when the church will have to decide about the nature of its ecumenical relationships with the Catholic, Episcopal, and Reformed churches. It will be interesting to watch what place the question of ordaining women receives.

What is clear from the Lutheran debate about ordaining women, however, is that without question it was Luther's attack on the sacramental system of the medieval church and its theology of ministry that made it possible for women to be ordained in 1970. Both churches appealed to the Lutheran notion of a functional ministry, one in which the focus is on the Word being spoken, not who the speaker is. While they may have come to regret their "functional" notion of the ministry for its lack of understanding of what the "office" established by Christ should be, their reasons are clear: The test of a good pastor, whether woman or man, has been and should continue to be whether one can preach the gospel of Jesus Christ clearly and with power. Women have shown themselves to be no better or worse at the task than men. That women can now preach and use their gifts for ministry to witness to the Lordship of Jesus Christ in public is a fact to be celebrated. *Soli Deo Gloria.*

Notes

1. Faculty minutes from Luther Seminary, December 5, 1958, p. 920.

2. *The Lutheran* 4 (July 20, 1966), p. 25.

3. Philip Heffner, "The Ministry of Women," *Lutheran Quarterly* 18, (May 1966), p. 102.

4. *The Lutheran* 4 (20 July 1966), p. 26.

5. Minutes from the Fourth Biennial Convention of the Lutheran Church in America, June 19-27, 1968, pp. 755-756.

6. "Report on Ordination of Women," Reports and Actions of the Fifth General Convention of the American Lutheran Church, October 21-27, 1970, p. 327.

7. Exhibit G, Page 8, Findings of March 1969, Minutes from the Annual Meeting of the Lutheran Council of the United States of America, February 3-4, 1970, p. 8.

8. Margaret Barth Wold, "We Seized the Spirit's Moment," *Lutheran Women in Ordained Ministry 1970-1995: Reflections and Perspectives* (Minneapolis: Augsburg Books, 1995), pp. 15-20.

9. Dorothy J. Marple, "God at Work among Us," *Lutheran Women in Ordained Ministry 1970-1995: Reflections and Perspectives* (Minneapolis: Augsburg Books, 1995), pp. 21-27.

10. "Report on Ordination of Women," Reports and Actions of the Fifth General Convention of the American Lutheran Church, October 21-27, 1970, pp. 429-430.

11. "President's Report," Reports and Actions of the Fifth General Convention of the American Lutheran Church, October 21-27, 1970, p. 141.

12. Mary Todd, "Now Is the Kairos—The Right Time," *Lutheran Women in Ordained Ministry 1970-1995: Reflections and Perspectives* (Minneapolis: Augsburg Books, 1995), pp. 28-32.

MY STORY, OUR STORY
Elizabeth Platz

ON NOVEMBER 22, 1970, many people came together on the occasion of my ordination to the holy ministry of Word and sacrament. Many of them were there in person. All were with me in spirit. This is their story too.

The preacher, Dr. Donald Heiges, and I had started at Gettysburg Seminary together—he as the new president and I as a first-year student. I had come from a women's college, Chatham, that happily encouraged its students to pursue that which engaged their curiosity and captured their imagination. And so I found myself in Heiges's office in the fall of 1962. Encouraged by my college professors, I had planned to study systematic theology (then a major), naively unaware that Lutheran seminaries did not then offer such an avenue to women. I entered Gettysburg Seminary only to discover that Christian education was my assumed course of study. I tried it for a quarter, but didn't like it. I returned to Heiges's office asking how I could major in systematics.

Heiges was a man who saw possibilities, not barriers. "Well," said he, "why don't you take the bachelor of divinity program in which the systematic major is offered?" Three years? A Bachelor of Divinity? Wasn't that for men being called to the ministry? Not necessarily, for there were no seminary prohibitions for it as an academic course. "Of course," he added, "you will need to take all the requirements: preaching, pastoral care, and so forth."

So my course was set. I was sure that I had no desire to become a pastor, but I did want to study theology. Two years later, the question of internship arose; it was an option, strongly encouraged but not required. Given my non-interest in being a pastor, there was no strong need to pursue an internship and, as Heiges knew, there really was no place for me to go. But he opened another door. This one was service, during my senior year, with John Vannorsdall, then chaplain at Gettysburg College. What a wonderful gift.

Vannorsdall was a mentor like no other. From him I learned the model of the ministry of planting seeds. In the mobile, seeking, and secular environment that marks higher education (and now most of our communities), he asked, "Could I live with the hope of the sower and forego the satisfaction of seeing the seed grow?" Where one finds sustenance and encouragement is an important question in ministry. I have rejoiced in the wonder of this image of the sower—and bewailed it when the institutional church asks for statistics.

Nearing the end of my senior year in seminary, I finally considered my future. After all, systematics or no, one has to eat and earn a living. In those days pastors came to interview the seniors awaiting call. Heiges found the opportunity to tell me that I might not be all that welcome. And it was true. Pastor after pastor let me know, sometimes with gentlemanly tact, that he didn't want a woman with a degree in systematic theology in his parish, listening to his sermons. But lest I be discouraged, Heiges was ready to open the door to ministry in higher education. And so I found myself sitting in the University of Maryland Chapel, listening to him preach at my ordination. This is his story as well.

The service was my first opportunity to offer communion to my family. Mom and Dad, my sister Kathy, my brother-in-law David, my niece Amy Beth, and my Sunday school teacher Mrs. Esther Succop are at the heart of the story. My life has been rich with the love and care given in a close working-class neighborhood where everyone seems to have a say. Mom and Dad were always there, convinced that I could do whatever needed to be done. They had never attended college, but when the possibility of college came for me they said, "Of course, go." What we all had in mind was a teachers' college or church school where I might become a teacher or a nurse and, above all, later a happy wife and good mother. Then I had the opportunity to go to a women's college of some standing. There was no word of "You won't fit in," but rather "Of course, go. We're here with you." And when, as a college senior, I spoke of going to seminary, my folks said, "Of course, go." (Dad did tease, saying I probably couldn't get a job anyway.)

My parents' confidence and trust in me often far exceeded my own. Their love and support were never in question. So when I called home to talk about the possibility of being ordained, it was not surprising to hear, "Well, we've been wondering when you would." This love and support has continued, since my parents' death, to be expressed in my sister and her family. The family values of caring, thoughtfulness, dreaming, responsibility, support, and belonging make dreams in life possible.

The ordaining officer at my ordination was Paul Orso, president (later to be called bishop) of the Maryland Synod, LCA. He was a door opener. Recognizing that because of unusual circumstances, a legislative synod convention was scheduled for the fall, he spent time seeing that all examining committee requirements and all processes were addressed. But this was not as significant to me as his support in talking through what it might mean to be a pastor. There were no models except male. It was a time of pants suits and strident voices. What did this mean when it came to being a pastor: pseudo-male, genderless, what?

Orso helped me see that there was no need for an apology for my gender, no need to assume characteristics of the male gender, and no need to assert my femaleness as the primary reason for ordination. In other words, he taught me to "act like you belong, for you do." It was an invaluable understanding that helped steer a course among other people's agendas, my own fears, and the wonder of the pastorate.

My colleagues in and outside the synod offered many gifts for my ordination: prayers, support, cartoons, encouragement. Leon Haines, secretary of the synod, saw that "brother" on the ordination certificate was obliterated and a beautiful calligraphic "sister" took its place. Amidst all these gifts there did come the ugliness of letters and phone calls describing me as an instrument of Satan, the whore of Babylon, and other expressions of fear and anger. The overwhelming care offered me was a rich antidote to such wounding behavior. Such care continues.

My stole came to me from the hands of a colleague with whom I had already shared five years of ministry. Ted Caspar and his wife Betty have shared their lives with me and their joy of exploring the beautiful in word and art, from medieval drama to contemporary poetry, from banner design to the wondrous decorations of a Lucia Fest, a Scandinavian festival of light played out in the darkness of winter. To care enough for others that you try to surround people with beauty, to free the imagination, to care for and encourage the individual—this is a gift you keep unpacking.

The presiding minister was not accustomed to wearing a chasuble—and a seventies one it was with glowing colors and butterflies. Gil Doan, regional director for National Lutheran Campus Ministry, is a central character of my story. He would become a mentor for me, teaching respect for the use of the mind, the pursuit of understanding, the unique worth of each person. Over the years Doan would invest himself in helping me sort out what it meant to do Word and sacrament ministry on campus. Love and respect are two words that I always associate with him. He is the mark of the many campus ministry colleagues who with generosity share themselves and their talents to encourage and excite something very special when your daily work is not always in a friendly environment and always under severe budget constraints.

The presence of Pastor Arnold Keller, dean of the conference, is a sign of the give-and-take of collegiality. Any pastor has the option to withdraw from collegial activities. What a mistake. As a non-parish pastor, often I have not been included in the thoughts and plans for the collegium, but persistence and presence have brought wonderful friendships and a broader world. I need to be held accountable and challenged by my colleagues and the possibilities of the larger community. The aloneness that can come with ministry can be met by collegiality.

ELIZABETH PLATZ

And collegiality marked the presence of the final partner in the laying-on of hands. The chairman of the ecumenical chapel staff and an Episcopal priest, Wofford Smith, took part in the laying-on of hands at a time when his own church did not ordain women. Methodist, Baptist, Presbyterian, and Roman Catholic colleagues were all present. With sharp wit and dry humor, they would prod at my Lutheran theology, inviting dialogue and clarity. At the death of each of my parents, colleagues traveled to Pittsburgh to be with me. Smith and the chapel colleagues helped me relinquish the need to defend my ordination, and be free of the chip on my shoulder placed there by my insecurity and the agendas of others. With Smith I would celebrate the mid-weekly Eucharist for twenty years. He would be an example of one who strives to discern justice and speak for those who cannot be heard. In time, after many years, this best friend became my beloved husband. His death has not ended his presence. My story would be incomplete without him.

The lessons were read by the chancellor of the university and a faculty member. Students served as ushers. The seminary choir sang from the balcony. This service was a confluence of forces that still shape my life twenty-five years later. Students, faculty, and staff shared their lives with me. The stumbling blocks and joys of a large university and an institutional church have been part of my everyday life. How to minister, to listen and grow, to be grace-full; to speak the Word; to be Christ to my neighbor; to be the church in a world where that is often suspect; not to forget all whom I am called to serve—students, groundskeepers, faculty, secretaries, administrators, graduate students, my fellow pastors, and ministries, congregations, and committees of the church—all these questions tumbled in some form through my mind at the service that day and continue to do so today.

The core story was present before me as I looked at the altar— bread and wine—Christ given and shed for you, for me. This is the call. Why was I ordained? Why should I be ordained? I was a fully qualified lay minister with good academic credentials doing programming, counseling, administration. I was happy.

How does one articulate the call? It is a many-petalled rose. There was the "tug" of the Eucharist. Each time it was celebrated there was the haunting feeling of being drawn to its mystery, but somehow also to responsibility. There was the incompleteness in working with students and faculty. One could counsel but the completion of offering confession and absolution, of blessing a wedding, of bringing the sacrament was not there. This was not and is not due to some artificial structure imposed by the church. It is a recognition that there is a ministry established by Christ that clearly and freely bears the responsibility of being a visible instrument for the support, nurture, and healing of God's children. The word *seelsorge,* the care of souls, became a reality for me. But it was not just mine to decide. Such responsibility carries authority (please note, not authoritarianism).

On November 20, 1970 I was Beth Platz. A student came by the office and asked for the pastor. I met him, let him know who I was, but he really wanted to see the pastor. On November 25, 1970 I was now Pastor Platz. A student came by and asked to see the pastor. "She is here," said the receptionist. "She?" said the confused fellow. "I didn't know we had women pastors. Can I talk to her?" and in he came.

It was not a question of my decision, it was not a question of my gender. It is a matter of trust that gives authority, of trust in an office, not an individual; of seeing in one designated by the church a repose and help. The call is an act of the church entrusting to one it has come to know the gifts of shepherding. It is a gift that cannot be forced on one. It is not a gift that can be demanded. It is the call to service. When our community says "pastor," it offers a trust and an expectation. The story is not mine:

> Elizabeth A. Platz has been duly approved by the Maryland Synod of the Lutheran Church in America on the twenty-fourth day of October, 1970 in session at Baltimore as one to whom the Ministry of the Gospel should be committed. By direction of the Church, therefore, I present her for Ordination to the Holy Ministry.

My service of ordination took place twenty-five years ago. The realities embodied in it are ever new. Preaching the Word and administering the sacraments form my life. They are the responsibilities particularly entrusted to me. The core of the story is brought to focus in the mystery of the Sacrament: an awesome, gracious God broken and given for new life. My story can but flow from this and it is not my story alone. There have been central and powerful figures, only a few of whom I have mentioned. There are many whom I shall never know who have made a story of a woman pastor possible: our grandmothers in the faith, scores of faithful deaconesses often lost in the telling of our story, the women of the church serving for generations, the countless hours of discussion, committee work, and exemplary ministry done by women lay leaders and church staff, all preparing the ground for such inclusion.

From the baptismal liturgy is the powerful identifying phrase, "[Elizabeth], child of God. . . ." To be God's child, to continue to explore what that might mean, to hear of one's uniqueness and worth, to be given the curiosity and courage to open doors, and to know the strength that phrase contains are but a few of the things I have learned from these words.

"Act like you belong, for you do" was a statement shared with me in my early years as part of an explanation of God's call and the possibilities inherent in God's promises. It has helped me as a woman pastor, as a single person in the church, as a pastor on campus, as a non-parish pastor in the synod, as the only woman on many committees.

"Lift up your hearts . . ." heralds the ever new and invigorating entrance to the Eucharist. To be able to issue this invitation, to be an instrument in offering this gift is a blessing at each celebration. To hear the words "given for you" and "shed for you," to be able to offer them is an honor offered to those chosen to serve as pastors. This is my story. *Soli Deo Gloria.*

BARBARA ANDREWS
Susan Thompson

BARBARA ANDREWS, the first woman ordained in the American Lutheran Church, is not here to reflect on that experience. She died seventeen years ago. Yet her brief ministry encouraged and inspired many, including this writer, a lay woman who was grateful to call Barbara friend.

I first met Barbara Andrews in October 1972, when a small group of women gathered in Minneapolis before the opening of the biennial convention of the American Lutheran Church (ALC). We had gathered to discuss a document that was to come before the convention entitled "Women and Men in Church and Society: Towards Wholeness in the Christian Community." The paper was both a reflection of changes happening in society and an effort to assist the church to understand, participate in, and provide leadership to efforts to foster the full utilization of God's gifts.

I had been eager to meet the Reverend Barbara L. Andrews for almost two years. On December 22, 1970, two months after the ALC had approved the ordination of women, Andrews had become the first woman ordained in that church body. The woman I saw that night was a little person with a big twinkle in her eyes. She wore a clerical collar and sat in a wheelchair. Those two distinguishing features were marks of her life, witness, ministry, and contribution to the church.

Andrews remarked that night that if the church was serious about the decision to ordain women, and believed that women also have the full ability to minister, it probably wouldn't have been necessary to bring the statement we were discussing to the next convention. Change of such scope usually doesn't happen fast. But when the movement towards women's ordination was brewing in the ALC, Andrews was ready. While serving on the staff of the Lutheran Campus Ministry at the University of Minnesota—St. Paul Campus from 1962 to 1969, she had studied at Luther Theological Seminary. During most of that time, she was one of only three women in the Master of Divinity program in a church body that did not yet ordain women. She was graduated in 1969, intending to seek ministry opportunities in health-care chaplaincy. She subsequently requested certification for ordination, stating "I have discovered that the hospital chaplaincy for which I seem most talented and most qualified may require [ordination]."[1] On October 1, 1969, in a letter announcing the Luther Seminary faculty action to certify Andrews for ordination, seminary president Dr. Alvin N. Rogness called Barbara "a very able student and deeply dedicated person." He continued, "Though the Faculty cannot make any judgment as to the place she will fulfill in the Church, we find her in character and in training prepared for ordination."[2]

A year later the ALC voted to authorize the ordination of women. Within two months Barbara Andrews had received and accepted a call to serve as assistant pastor at Edina Community Lutheran Church, in Edina, Minnesota. The Reverend James Siefkes, preacher at her ordination, said that day, "You came rolling through the door, Barbara, and you pushed it open for all the women who will follow you. The door will not close again."[3] It has not and it will not. And now the doors moved through by Pastor Andrews, and the Reverend Elizabeth Platz, ordained by the Lutheran Church in America one month earlier, have been entered by more than 1700 women. The Evangelical Lutheran Church in America Division for Ministry report stated that in 1994 more than forty percent of the students enrolled in Lutheran seminaries were women.[4] Two synodical bishops are women. Women serve in ordained and lay positions, salaried and volunteer, throughout the church in capacities and numbers far beyond what was imaginable only a few decades ago.

Barbara Andrews was born on May 11, 1935 in Minneapolis, Minnesota, with cerebral palsy. She lived her life in a wheelchair that she did not have the strength to propel. Her mobility and personal needs were provided for first by her family and other caregivers and later by her friends. With determination and courage she built and rebuilt her support network. Friends remember the "luggers," men and women who pushed Andrews around campus during her undergraduate years at Gustavus Adolphus College, as well as at the University of Minnesota and Luther Seminary. Her wheelchair was both a symbol and a result of the effect of her birth circumstances on her entire life, personal and professional. Andrews felt that for some people, the wheelchair provided an excuse to avoid taking her seriously as a woman in ministry.

Andrews lived and worked before there was a history of women clergy in the Lutheran church. She also lived and worked at the dawn of efforts to make more possible the full functioning of disabled people in the educational and employment mainstream in this country. She embodied consciousness-raising on several fronts. Pastor Arvid Dixen, who ordained Andrews and with whom she served in her first parish, said of her, "She was an incredible visual aid for us on women ordained, and on ministry to, with, and of the disabled."[5] Dr. Carl Thomas, Executive Director of Lutheran Social Services of Michigan, spoke similarly of her commitment to the total ministry of the church. "She cared deeply about congregations and their welfare," he said, "and she had dreams of their future in relating to both women pastors and the disabled."[6]

Andrews was, in addition, a person shaped by the particular gifts God gave her. She clearly had experienced physical suffering and had a heart for the suffering of others. In her second call, where she served as a nursing home chaplain, the frail elderly were most accustomed to a pastor who stood by their beds. In Andrews they found a pastor who was physically frail herself and who sat by their bedsides, sharing with them God's love for all people. Andrews' playfulness and joy in God's love were other ministry gifts to which people responded well, especially children who found in her an adult who spoke to them eye to eye.

Andrews even did her best to bring lightheartedness into her mobility challenges. She chuckled at being called a "Holy Roller," and at being swung around the dance floor at campus ministry events.

Andrews was also a good listener and keen analyst of human behavior. Perhaps those skills were enhanced by her lack of mobility and resultant position of observer some of the time. Whatever its source, her perceptivity served her well as pastor and friend. When I once attributed a personal mistake to my ethnic background, Andrews immediately responded, "It's all right to say 'I'm this way because I'm Norwegian.' But when are you going to quit blaming it on being Norwegian and do something about it?" I sensed then and do now the experience out of which those words came. Their challenge to act positively, not simply explain negatively, has come back to me many times over the years.

Crucial to Andrews' life, and to her life as a pastor, was her reliance on God's tender care. Dixen recalls the day he waited tensely at the hospital for word about his newborn son's possible heart problem. Andrews rolled into the room and said, "Don't worry, Jesus and I will take care of you."[7] He recalls sensing in a new way the profound truth of those words he had so often used himself.

Andrews' grit and sense of independence in the face of the enormous efforts it took to function day by day, become educated, and be taken seriously in ministry are also common threads in the recollections of people who knew her well. Siefkes remembers, "She had a strong sense of call to ordained ministry and acted upon it, despite the obstacles."[8] Grit and independence were surely lived out in Andrews' acceptance of a call in 1974 from Lutheran Social Services of Michigan to serve as chaplain at Luther Haven Nursing Home in Detroit. That move meant leaving her lifelong home base and support system in Minneapolis to accept the challenge of self-sufficiency in a new city. Since Abraham and Sarah, unknown numbers have moved on to an uncertain future in response to God's call. But to do it with the level of physical dependence with which Barbara

Andrews lived required an extra degree of determination and courage.

Andrews did make the transition to her new call and to living on her own in Detroit. After two and a half years, she resigned the call at Lutheran Social Services and subsequently served as interim pastor at Resurrection Lutheran Church in Detroit. On March 31, 1978, Andrews died in a fire in her apartment. Her determination and courage were evident even then by indications that she had been working to put out the fire when she was overcome by asphyxiation. It was the end of an often difficult, sometimes lonely, and in many ways heroic life.

Andrews is not here to share her experiences firsthand, or to reflect on them with us as we observe the twenty-fifth anniversary of Lutheran women in ordained ministry. We rely on friends and colleagues who remember her for who she was: a whole person, gifted but burdened, gentle yet able to confront. They recall the difficulties she endured and the difficulty they had sometimes in meeting her high expectations and wonder how much the former led to the latter. Surely those of us who are able-bodied can only guess at the toll of constantly having to manage or arrange for life activities as basic as getting from place to place, speaking loudly enough to be heard, providing for daily living and personal care that she was unable to do alone. Most cannot know the impact of life in a wheelchair on a woman in a culture so historically focused on woman's appearance as a source of her value. Perhaps no one can fully understand the effect of those experiences in the additional light of being not only an ordained Lutheran minister, but the first ordained woman in her church body.

The desire to be fully employed, for both vocational and financial reasons, also provided problems for Andrews at times. She had been a member of the congregation that ultimately called her to serve as a pastor and she was well liked and respected there. The secret ballot to call her as assistant pastor part-time was unanimously affirmative. Yet while even her part-time salary may have pushed the congregation's abilities, it could not cover her needs. In addition to the usual living expenses, Andrews' cost of living was compounded by the need for personal assistance and the need to travel by taxi, partly in fulfillment of her visitation ministry. In order to manage financially, Andrews received government assistance during this period.

The obstacles in Andrews' life were many. Her warmth, love, and personal courage are an important aspect of what drew people to her. The demands she at times made may in fact have been necessary to her survival, her accomplishments, and ultimately her ministry.

✳✳✳

The way of women clergy was not easy in the beginning and is not always smooth today. There were those who thought that the ordination and ministry of Barbara Andrews would not prove to be trail-blazing for other women because her disability made her situation unique. The fact is that the example of Barbara Andrews as the first woman pastor in the ALC was another of God's many gifts to the church throughout the centuries. That Andrews accepted the "fishbowl" challenge of being the first woman ordained in the ALC, and that she did live her call under the additional demands of her disability, left a remarkable legacy of hope, determination, commitment, and faith in God's grace to all who would follow her.

Barbara Andrews had an unusual measure of mental and intellectual strength. She had a major physical disability. She was playful and fun-loving. She had a tenacity and single-mindedness that at times got her through and at other times created barriers between herself and others. She appreciated recognition but might have said, "Oh, come on now" at words of admiration in this essay. Andrews could be both serious and tender, as relationships or pastoral situations dictated. She was, most of all, a child of God and a gift of God.

On January 5, 1995, Barbara Andrews was posthumously awarded the Faithfulness in Ministry Cross by Luther Seminary.

Notes

1. ELCA Archives, Barbara Andrews' letter to Dr. Olaf Hanson, Dean of Faculty, Luther Theological Seminary, undated, Exhibit A.

2. ELCA Archives, Alvin Rogness' letter to The Rev. Herbert Nottbohm, of ALC Church Council certifying Barbara Andrews for ordination, (October 14, 1969), Exhibit B.

3. James Siefkes, interview with author, phone conversation, January 25, 1990.

4. ELCA enrollment statistics compiled annually by the Division for Ministry.

5. Arvid Dixen, interview with author, phone conversation, January 25, 1990.

6. Carl Thomas, interview with author, phone conversation, January 22, 1990.

7. Dixen interview, January 25, 1990.

8. Siefkes interview, January 25, 1990.

Portions of this article were first printed in the June 1990 issue of *Lutheran Woman Today*.

BREAKING AWAY
Janith Maureen Otte

IT WAS 1971 and I was just out of college, in my early twenties. I had been teaching theology and history at Lutheran High South in St. Louis, Missouri, since the fall of 1969. During the summer of 1970, I had started taking classes in the Master of Arts in Religion (M.A.R.) program at Concordia Seminary, St. Louis. I was sitting with a friend on the front steps outside my apartment, one block from the seminary. We spoke about the political situation in The Lutheran Church–Missouri Synod (LCMS), the recent decisions of the Lutheran Church in America and the American Lutheran Church to ordain women, the fact that LCMS was not even considering women's ordination, and that there were no women Master of Divinity (M.Div.) candidates at the seminary.

Somewhere in the course of that conversation, or shortly thereafter, I made the decision to change direction at the seminary and to enroll in the M.Div. program. I made this decision because I loved the church and I wanted to be ordained. I felt women should have the same choices and opportunities as men. I was angry that the Missouri Synod was so unfair, so patriarchal, so rigid, and so closed. I thought the church had an obligation to deal with this issue, and I wanted to be part of creating that change within the church.

By 1972 I was enrolled in the M.Div. program at the seminary, taking classes and adjusting to the life of being a full-time student again. I became engrossed in my studies and loved the intellectual stimulation. I had great professors and the seminary was alive with the spirit of change and political intrigue. It was a special time and my hopes were high.

At the same time, the reality of the situation began to sink in more deeply. I was completely surrounded by men. The perspectives were male. I was told by various seminary administrators that I probably would *not* get a teaching parish, that I probably would *not* be able to go out on internship (or vicarage, as we called it), that I would *not* be certified for ministry, and that ordination was out of the question. Ordinary privileges that the male students took for granted were withheld from me and had to be argued for and justified. Each of these steps or decisions required great debate, discussion, many meetings, and paperwork to champion making any changes regarding women's ordination.

I started feeling as though I had to explain who I was, what I thought, and what I wanted. I began to feel not good enough as I was. I was filled with such incredible rage and yet I knew that if I ever allowed myself to get angry enough to express my feelings I would jeopardize my dreams and ambitions. I was very aware that I had no political leverage or power and that I was dependent on the goodwill of at least some of these men. And so I made the decision to repress my feelings and quiet my voice. I adopted a public persona of being strong, competent, unfazed, able to handle anything. In effect, I turned myself inside out to get through the program. I wish now that I could have expressed my feelings regardless of circumstances and consequences. I would have said, "This is stupid. This is wrong. This is unfair. There is absolutely no acceptable reason for making me jump through these hoops. I deserve the same privileges as any male seminarian."

The student body at the seminary consisted of almost nine hundred men. There were two women in the M.A.R. program and I was the only woman in the M.Div. program during my first year. What that meant was that women's voices were few and far between. It was clearly the male voice that predominated. Women were silencing their voices to be accepted.

JANITH MAUREEN OTTE

The male seminarian's responses and behaviors ranged from openness, which was expressed in a willingness to learn what it meant to be the only woman in this very male system, to hostility, which was expressed in withdrawal or disdain. In class I was sometimes called upon to voice "the woman's reality." I didn't know what that was. I was having a hard enough time just trying to figure out what I thought most of the time. Outside of class, I was pointed out by students to their parents as "the woman M.Div. student."

Being on display as the token female was very painful. I started to feel self-conscious and trapped by the assumptions of others. The men seemed to expect me to know everything, to be everything, to speak for all women. Any internal questions or doubts were discouraged. I was constantly competing to prove myself, to show that I was as good as any man in the program. I began to feel alone and more isolated. Always having to prove my worth became a major painful theme throughout my years of study.

During this time I experienced a deep sense of betrayal. I had expected that there would be a sense of belonging, of total acceptance, especially at the seminary. I had imagined that the setting would resemble that of a healthy family or community where persons are encouraged to be who they are and supported in their efforts. The church and the seminary held the greatest promise of this for me. In reality, however, these institutions were the source of some of my biggest disappointments, as more and more I felt I had to pretend and hide. It felt very much as if I were back in my dysfunctional family as a child growing up. It didn't feel safe to be myself and I began to withdraw behind the role I was assigned. The church community became yet another dysfunctional environment and mimicked so many of the dysfunctional families of my generation.

As a psychotherapist, I know now that people generally choose conditions that will give them what they didn't get in their early life. It's their attempt to fill the void. Naturally then, I was searching for a healthy community where I would be accepted for who I was. The major disappointment was always having to play a particular role representing the church and rarely being able to relax into my own ideas, thoughts, and feelings. I felt more like a puppet than a person. There seemed to be no room for individuation and the path of acceptance was extremely narrow.

Having left Concordia Seminary in 1974 over a number of issues, including the issue of women's ordination, I graduated from Concordia Seminary in Exile (Seminex) in May 1976.[1] During my internship in my fourth year, I served at the University Lutheran Chapel in Berkeley, California and Kairos, a residential counseling program for young women in Oakland. After graduation, I returned to California where I continued to work at the University Chapel and Kairos.

Being in the Bay Area, I was surrounded by other women and some men from whom I felt support, especially political support. Together we advocated for women's ordination and participated in the formation of the Association of Evangelical Lutheran Churches (AELC).[2] However, as the only female graduate from Seminex and the focus of the ordination debate, I was keenly aware of being the "role model." I began to feel responsible not just for myself, but for all women. Because I wanted women to see a woman functioning in this role and because I felt the female perspective had to be heard, I felt pressure always to be involved and act appropriately. It became more and more difficult to say no to requests for a female voice or presence. Once again, I lost myself completely to this role. I no longer knew who I was apart from the role I played.

In October 1977, I received a joint call from the University Lutheran Chapel in Berkeley and the Pacific Regional Synod of the AELC. I was ordained on Reformation Sunday, October 30, 1977, at St. Paulus Lutheran Church in San Francisco.

Following my ordination I continued to be very busy, traveling quite a bit, serving on numerous regional and national boards, commissions or committees. I preached, wrote position papers, helped organize women, and sat in meetings. Some of this was necessitated by the fact that even though the Pacific Regional Synod of the AELC had ordained me, the AELC had not yet made a decision regarding women's ordination. The debate persisted.

I continued to work for another five years, but I was becoming numb to my surroundings. I was going through the motions, but internally I was exhausted, burned out, depleted. I felt as though I was dying, having sacrificed my feelings and any personal identity I had known before. Feeling totally disconnected from myself, I often contemplated suicide.

In desperation and with enormous guilt, I resigned my position as associate pastor of University Lutheran Chapel in December 1981. The chapel council asked if there was anything that could be done to make me reconsider. At that point, I didn't have the ability or energy to give the question an appropriate response or even to negotiate terms.

After my resignation, I heard from no one else in the church, official or otherwise. My marriage was disintegrating during this period and eventually ended in divorce. No one seemed to care! I felt isolated. I made no attempts to contact anyone because I felt guilty. I welcomed my solitude for I didn't want to be accountable to anyone. The whole situation felt like a failure.

In the mid-1980s, after being on the inactive roster for several years, I officially resigned from the clergy roster. I wanted to be free to reclaim myself, to heal. Leaving the ordained ministry seemed to be the only way I could do that. Since all experiences can be used as opportunities for learning, there are a number of lessons I have gathered from my years at the seminary, from being ordained and from leaving. I now consider these experiences invaluable for how I live my life.

To begin with, these experiences gave me the impetus to start the process of confronting the past and some very painful and deeply buried feelings of my childhood that unfortunately were so similar to my seminary experiences. I had reached a point in my life where I was willing to do whatever it took to deal with my feelings and to heal from old wounds. I was determined to find and be my authentic self.

Confronting these feelings, I learned that I cannot develop in a system that is closed, rigid, and patriarchal. I need a healthy community and family around me to support my continued efforts to be emotionally honest and truthful. It's not enough to be around people who tolerate feelings. I need people who truly respect and honor them, and who see them as an integral part of their lives. The respectful process of how we are with ourselves and others is more important than the content or the outcome.

No external authority, the church or the seminary, can bestow identity on me or tell me how I feel. I have learned to treasure my thoughts and feelings and respect my life experiences, making my own conclusions and identifying my truths as I go along.

I learned that the church is not able to give me a personal experience with God or even the trust that God is operating in my life. Reading books, attending classes, going to church cannot create or give me that sense of spirituality. Ironically, only after leaving the ordained ministry and learning to trust myself did I also begin to trust that God is truly working in my life.

And finally, I learned that when a person represses emotional responses to life experiences, she or he will develop serious physical ailments. It is the body's way of speaking and trying to get our attention. As a child living in a repressed environment I developed asthma, occasional boils on my face, and scoliosis (a curvature of the spine). At seminary where I felt the need to suppress feelings, I developed adult acne. No medication or remedy had any lasting effect. I was not living in my own skin. And my scoliosis got worse. Doctors said that I would probably require surgery to avoid further deterioration of the spine. Years later, after I began to seriously address my feelings and emotional needs, my body began to show the results of living my life more honestly. My scoliosis has not gotten worse, contrary to medical opinion. My skin has cleared. At the time of this writing, however, all of the pain from the past resurfaced and my skin did break out. It has since cleared up.

Upon leaving the church, I have discovered a sense of God in my life, my true voice, and a healthier body. What changes have to be made for others like myself to find their way back to the church? It is time for those changes to happen and it is altogether possible.

JANITH MAUREEN OTTE

Notes

1. Mary Todd, "Now Is the Kairos—The Right Time," *Lutheran Women in Ordained Ministry 1970-1995: Reflections and Perspectives* (Minneapolis: Augsburg Books, 1995), pp. 28-32.
2. *Ibid.*

HARVEST OF GRACE: WOMEN IN RURAL MINISTRY

Stephanie K. Frey

THE PLACES WHERE we live and work change us. Landscapes work their way into the mind's eye, shaping our sense of space, our view of the horizon, our notion of beauty. People change us as well by what they say and do, think, feel, and believe. In the past fifteen years, I have been changed by the prairie landscape of southwestern Minnesota and eastern South Dakota, and by being in the company of rural people while serving internship, two congregational calls, and now a call to the synod staff in a rural synod.

Accustomed to the rolling, wooded hills of southern Wisconsin where I grew up, my eye has now been trained for the long view that the prairie affords. My senses have become attuned to the plainer beauty of these open spaces. This is where soybeans and corn are planted row upon row, and ditches are filled with prairie grasses and wild sage. Here creeks and rivers curve with abandon through the humanly-devised orderliness of fence lines and the square-mile divisions of fields. It is a landscape that can be harsh with summer storms and winter snows, and yet can sustain the fragile bloom of the pasqueflower when the ground thaws in early spring.

More important, of course, there are people who must be spoken of here. The experience I have had in ministry among rural people has been nothing less than a harvest of grace. For me, this ministry began with the people of Colton Lutheran Parish in Colton, South Dakota, where I served my internship. Arriving there in 1980, I was the first female intern, but not the last. The people of the Colton parish showed me a gracious welcome, even those who may have harbored doubts about the whole idea of female pastors.

Parish leaders were quietly concerned, I think, about the program they had established over the years to acquaint interns with rural life and farming practices. Interns spent a day each month with dairy farmers, livestock feeders, crop farmers, or grain elevator managers. Folks wondered whether I, as a woman and a city kid, would want to participate in such things. When they discovered that I was interested (who wouldn't want to ride in a combine, after all!), their reticence disappeared and a marvelous year of learning was underway, with a seasoned pastor and the people of the two congregations as my teachers.

Even with its many joys, rural ministry has not been easy at every turn. There have been moments, as a newcomer to small-town life, when it felt as though being single, female, and ordained was such an anomaly that people did not quite know what to make of me. Rural communities can be closed communities, due to the fact that many families have lived in the same town or on the same family farm for generations. People who have been in town twenty-five or thirty years may still be considered outsiders, because they weren't born there. In such settings, the itinerant nature of pastors' lives is more evident than ever, for we are never finally insiders.

Some of my female colleagues, particularly those from urban backgrounds, have found these aspects of rural life more isolating and frustrating than has been healthy to bear. For others, however, rural parishes have been places where our ministries have been willingly received. We have been sustained by faithful people who demonstrated the gospel to us in such a way that we were given hope and energy for the tasks of preaching, teaching, and pastoral care.

Our calls to agricultural communities have also offered us the chance to live among people whose lives are more authentically seasonal than what we have experienced in the city. As farm work and other aspects of rural life revolve around seed time and harvest, there are changes in the pace of work throughout the year. Rural ministry is demanding because most pastors do not have the luxury of specialized "portfolios," but attend to the whole spectrum of ministry tasks.

Nevertheless, the pace is not quite as frenetic as it can be elsewhere. For women who desire to have their lives constituted of more things than our work, rural congregations and an open landscape provide what one friend calls "room to breathe."

RURAL WOMEN AS MODELS FOR MINISTRY

It is not possible to speak of my experience of rural ministry without also speaking of the women I came to know in each congregation who modeled ministry in their daily lives. On nearly every Wednesday morning of my internship year, for instance, I had coffee with the ten to fifteen women who gathered in the church basement to make quilts for Lutheran World Relief. They were strong and capable women. Sturdy in spirit, their lives were examples of hard work, creativity, dedication, and frequent partnership with their husbands in farming or other businesses in the community.

The sum of experiences and abilities present in these women was vast. One woman had an infant or toddler with her nearly every week, because she and her husband had been foster parents to over seventy little ones even as they raised their own family. Another woman was the one who, on a fresh spring morning, excitedly took me to a section of untilled prairie west of town on which the pasqueflowers bloomed. She was an artist, and when my internship was over she presented me with a framed arrangement of those and other wild flowers she had dried so I might remember my prairie year. Another, in her eighties, was quiet and shy, but lavishly presented us weekly with freshly-made *lefse* and *kringla*, Scandinavian delicacies. As these quilters broke from their work at midmorning, I was blessed with their conversation and stories. It soon became clear that the long history of their skillful lay leadership within the church had paved the way for those of us being called to take a new direction and pursue ordination. It was among these women that my own sense of call to ordained ministry was confirmed, and it was from them, especially the oldest among them, that I received the strongest vocational and personal support. "More power to you!" said one eighty-five year old in her Christmas greeting, "It thrills me to see you up there preaching."

WOMEN AS BEARERS OF THE FAITH

The apostle Paul acknowledged Timothy's mother Eunice and grandmother Lois as faith-bearers for each successive generation (2 Timothy 1:5). Women still are frequently the ones who take primary responsibility within families for passing on the heritage of Christian faith to their children. This is evident in rural communities as well, where the long hours kept by men who were farming often left the women alone to attend to the teaching of Bible stories, hymns, and prayers to the children. Several colleagues and I have wondered about whether the matriarchal leaning in this aspect of life might influence the ways men in rural congregations relate to female pastors. Each of us could think of men who talked loudly against the ordination of women, but over time became people who conversed with us at length, more openly than they were willing to do with other men. In the end, these men became genuine supporters of our ministry. Perhaps in us they saw and heard their own mothers and grandmothers who were bearers of the faith—and so spoke freely, discovering along the way that the politics of this new thing quickly dissolved as they came to know us, and as they needed a pastor in difficult times.

There are wonderful stories to be told of the ways men in our congregations have shown us their care and esteem. Often this takes the form of finding and completing tasks such as lawn mowing, snow shoveling, or scraping car windows of frost in midwinter after a long late-night council meeting. Early on, I found some of these gestures patronizing ("I can take care of myself," I thought). A friend tells of a Sunday morning when she had to drive the fifteen miles to her country church after a heavy nighttime snowfall. When she turned slowly onto Town Line Road, she came upon a parishioner waiting in the county snowplow he operated. He knew what time she usually arrived at that corner on her way to worship each week, and so he had waited there. He drove ahead of her, clearing the path so she could drive safely. When they made it to the next plowed highway, he pulled over, climbed out of the cab, tipped his hat as she passed him, and continued his morning's work.

Another man in that same parish had taken it as his job each Sunday to put a glass of fresh water in the pulpit for the pastor. One terrible week, the man's wife was struck by a truck and killed as she crossed the road in front of their farm to get the mail. My friend was called immediately to that gruesome scene, where she wept and prayed with this man and his family. The funeral was on Saturday afternoon. Early the next day, as she was in the sacristy preparing for worship, she heard this man's distinctive gait on the steps coming up from the church basement. There he was, cup of water in hand. Amazed to see him so few hours after burying his wife, she asked, "What are you doing here?" "Where else would I be?" he replied.

Now, in later years, I have learned simply to receive these gestures as the acts of kindness and caring that they are. They are gifts these individuals have to give to their pastor, evidence of their affection and respect not only for us as persons, but also for the office of ministry.

WHAT SHAKES THE TREE?

Once when I commented to someone about how surprised I was that the most outspoken support for me as a female pastor came from older people, his reply was this: "Well, they've lived long enough to know what really shakes the tree and what doesn't—and ordaining women doesn't." I think that is true, and may reflect something central to rural life. Agriculture is a culture based on risk-taking. Year in and year out, farmers entrust their livelihoods to the risky business of putting seed to soil. In spite of farming practices that help reduce the risks, farmers cannot control the weather, so they must give over their concerns, waiting and watching. Perhaps it is this aspect of risk-taking that has allowed so many rural congregations to receive the ministry of women clergy with graciousness and welcome. Call committees may hesitate, people may speak against the notion, and some individuals may never come around in their thinking. Others, however, do change, and come to discover that the risk wasn't so great after all. The same kind of risk that leads to the harvest of the fields can lead to a harvest of grace in the congregation for both the pastor and the people she is privileged to serve.

SISTERS TOGETHER IN MINISTRY
Norma Cook Everist

WOMEN HAVE WITNESSED to the risen Christ since the open tomb. When Lutheran women were ordained in 1970, they joined the long procession of women proclaiming God's grace and ministering in Christ's name. The story of women's ordination is set in the context of the ministry of lay women, of women in religious orders, of women holding a variety of professional positions in the church. Contrary to perceptions that male clergy were now "letting" women in, "allowing" them to serve, a more historic view is that women would not be pastors today except for the commitment and support of lay women. The story of the contributions of these lay women that brought about change is told elsewhere is this volume. My story is set in the context of these faithful sisters, women in ministry always and everywhere. These women of faith believed call should be discerned on gifts, not gender, and changed the church.

ORDINATION IN THE MIDDLE OF MINISTRY

I was ordained in the middle of ministry. Fifty-five years ago I was baptized; thirty-five years ago I was consecrated a Lutheran deaconess. It was in my tenth year of diaconal ministry in suburban and urban settings that the American Lutheran Church (ALC) and Lutheran Church in America (LCA) voted to ordain women. Because the need for servanthood ministry is unlimited, I felt no urgency to seek ordination. The question for me was, "Could my ordination serve the church?"

On a hot summer day in the mid-1970s our Northeast Area Deaconess Conference, meeting at the home of one of our deaconesses in Bridgeport, Connecticut moved from the yard to the protecting shade of the garage. There I asked my sisters, "Should I seek ordination?" I did not need their permission but sought more than their advice. Women's religious communities, no longer under male clerical authority, shared leadership and mutual discernment. I received not only their blessing but their vision, "We need some deaconesses to help carry our heritage of servant leadership into this form of ministry."

Many people assumed, "Now that you are going on to higher things. . . ." That was not at all what we wanted to say. Why should a woman leave a community of women to serve in this office? And so I continue a deaconess to this day, using my particular gifts to serve as pastor and professor. Historically change is never unambiguous, usually painful as well as joyful, and always a lot of work. We choose to live the ambiguity in the midst of ministry.

Some people, in jest and in fear of ordaining a woman, asked, "How many more of you are out there?" There are over four hundred women in the Lutheran Deaconess Conference (more an order than an office), serving in a wide variety of ministries in various offices in the church and on behalf of the church in the world; twelve are ordained to pastoral ministry. Most women continue to serve as women always have and, in the middle of ministry, take on new challenges as well. In the middle of their ministry of going to anoint the dead Jesus, the women at the open tomb were called to change direction. They turned around to tell the news of life. They were still women.

SEEING OURSELVES IN EACH OTHER

Almost always in those early years when I preached or celebrated Eucharist in a congregation, parishioners saw a woman in these roles for the first time. I soon discovered that while women at the door after the service asked about me, before they finished their first sentence they were talking about themselves. Seeing a clergywoman did not make them more anxious, nor detract from their worship, but reflected their own ministries in a new light.

When I said, "Tell me about yourself," we could all imagine ministry in new ways.

When I taught at Yale Divinity School there were a number of women on the faculty. When I came to Wartburg Seminary in 1979, students had not seen a woman in a tenure-track position before. That first January interim I traveled with women students to visit women clergy in parish ministry. The students needed to see a variety of role models. We stayed overnight in their homes; women clergy were literally few and far between.

For centuries women's ministry was mostly unrecorded. As women prepared for ordained service, the temptation might be to learn male leadership styles and preaching stance, to interpret strength as mere fortitude. Likewise male mentors and supervisors might either abdicate this unfamiliar role or too eagerly try to disciple women in their image, thereby sabotaging women's growth and unwittingly turning them away from lay women. But women have sought and found women in all types of ministry as role models. This has, in turn, changed the seminaries.[1]

We may spin through revolving doors moving between male and female arenas. Those threatened by a woman exercising authority have frequently made provocative remarks to me when I preside at an ordination. I am comfortable in that place of formerly exclusively male power. I was equally comfortable when women invited me to peel potatoes with them the night before an ordination. I have always felt at home among lay women, whether admiring the vivid colors in a quilt, comparing business management styles, or updating each other on children. We need to study each other's ministry, seeing each other reflected there.

NOT ALLOWING OURSELVES TO BE DIVIDED

Many fears accompanied women's ordination. I often heard, "This will drive away the few men left in the church." Reaching inactive people remains a challenge, but women clergy did not drive men away. I also heard "Do you know who opposed her call?" with the questioner quickly adding, almost with delight, "Lay women!" Women's opposition to other women is often exaggerated, perhaps in fear of male exclusion or in discomfort with women bonding.

Women have often been divided from women: Sarah and Hagar, Rachel and Leah, Peninnah and Hannah, harlot and virgin, single and married, old and young, thin and fat, "working and non-working" (whatever that means: all women work), bad woman and good woman, clergy and lay, barren and childbearing. Whenever we allow ourselves to be defined in one-dimensional, divisive ways, we participate in our own self-diminishing and dismiss a sister in Christ.

There is much at stake in keeping women divided from women. What may begin like a compliment, "We're so proud of you," may have attached, "You're unlike most women who only. . . ." What may sound like genuine interest—"Tell me about your children"—may turn into, "I'm glad you're not like those career women who. . . ." In spite of unthinking, uncaring remarks or divisive comparisons, women have been able to move beyond the societal divisions; their gathering has been healing, natural, and energy-producing.

Although women of all ages and circumstances, at all stages of life, began and continue to come to seminary, for many the time of choice has passed. But women who say, "I might have . . ." celebrate with those who say, "I could." Before 1959 deaconesses could not marry. I was consecrated in 1960. Before 1970 Lutheran women in the U.S. could not be ordained. The date of an ecclesial decision divides women who are otherwise very similar. How amazing that, although (to use Luther's term) we have different stations in life that are often historically denied or proscribed by church and society, women reach across such restrictive divisions not in jealousy or judgment, but in empathy, mutual anguish, and joy.

During times of change it is easy to allow ourselves to be divided. Not only forms of ministry, but inclusive language, human sexuality issues, and redefined authority relationships challenge unity. Not only are church and society changing, but so are we. We no longer think as we used to and we may change still more. When someone is where I was yesterday or where I may be tomorrow, we may dismiss or threaten one another. We dare not allow ourselves to be divided again, or unfavorably compared one to another. At that very moment we need to stand by and support even the woman from whom such conversation would separate us. We need each other.

BEYOND TOKENISM TOWARD PARTNERSHIP

We have moved beyond the token stage. No longer am I necessarily the first woman to preside at the Eucharist in a congregation. No longer am I the only woman at a professors' conference. That's good, because the token stage is the most dangerous, for a number of reasons.

It is dangerous for the sole woman to consider herself or be considered unique (whether strange or special). Tokenism is dangerous because it is the time of greatest fear, the "What if . . ." stage. "What if all women now want to be ordained?" "What if they take over the church?" I experienced, not just once in a while, but virtually every time women gathered at the token stage, a man saying, "Oh, I see you are plotting to overthrow us," or "We'll have to break this up," usually jokingly, but pointedly.

As the Evangelical Lutheran Church in America (ELCA) lives into the representational principle promise in terms of race, gender, office, and age, those fears begin to fall away. Ironically the more women present, the less fear in the room. Now when we gather for synod assembly or task force meeting, the equal number of men and women feels natural; the occasional, almost exclusively male, official meeting now feels as unhealthy as it actually was. We need these guidelines to curb our propensity to move backward.

The token stage was dangerous for women in relation to women with the awkward decision to leave a women's group for token acceptance in a male professional group. We do need to meet in specific work groups, as associates in ministry, bishops, diaconal ministers, pastors, synodical women's organization leaders. Role clarity facilitates mutually accountable relationships. We also need to talk across role distinctions. Women clergy are part of Women of the ELCA. Sharing our gifts, ideas, our questions about each other is mutually supportive.[2]

WOMEN IN MINISTRY, ALWAYS AND EVERYWHERE

We commemorate twenty-five years of Lutheran women ordained and almost two thousand years of Christian women in ministry. Women entering the public ministry of pastor provides one more way to bridge the gap between public and private spheres, intensified during the nineteenth century and again after World War II.[3] Women, though relegated to the private sphere, always cared about children at home and around the world, about housekeeping and justice-seeking. Their insights—that war is tragic, not glorious, that people need to be fed in order to learn—are longstanding, but new is the realization that their voices as well as their ministry can and must prevail in places of power. If women and men participate as partners in the private and public spheres, might there be a different relationship, not only between men and women, but between the public and private spheres?

We also celebrate transformation of the concept of volunteer. Women ordained, as well as in many other public roles, does not mean demise of the volunteer but opportunities for men and women for truly volitional ministry. We are all free in Christ for vocation, callings to life sustaining ministries in all arenas of daily life. We see men caring for children, being secretary at meetings, serving in church kitchens and soup kitchens.

I have encountered women across this land in many ministries in daily life. A prison nurse in Washington state finds ways to care and touch in spite of AIDS restrictions. A mother in Colorado, through years of commitment and hard work, equips her daughter, in a wheelchair because of cerebral palsy, to be a minister herself as Sunday school superintendent, library worker, advocate with the governor for accessibility. An Iowa woman who volunteers in her community and church, statewide and churchwide, retires in Missouri and soon sees new challenges there for which her wise leadership is again required. A personnel manager for a large fast-food chain in Texas is a shepherd to the thousands she serves, knowing their names, equipping them, giving them choices, building their self-esteem. A telephone company customer service representative from Georgia listens to the agony in a man's questions when he's told he must shut off utilities and leave his home because flood waters are rising. Three women: social worker, educator, and pastor at Iglesia Luterana San Juan in Massachusetts, form a strong, gentle team of support and outreach in their neighborhood all week long. We celebrate women ministers since the open tomb, going to tell and serve every one.

Notes

1. Phyllis Anderson, "Lutheran Women in Theological Studies: Headway, Hard Work, Hurt, and Hope," *Lutheran Women in Ordained Ministry 1970-1995: Reflections and Perspectives* (Minneapolis: Augsburg Books, 1995), pp. 129-136.

2. An exhilarating example was in 1986 when the American Lutheran Church Women (ALC) Lutheran Church Women (LCA) and Women in Action for Mission (AELC) preparing to become one church and one Women of the ELCA, gathered at a number of locations around the country for two-day theological conferences with women. There were now-recognized women theologians who served as major presenters and women participated in many workshops. The level of theological discussion among lay and clergywomen was significant. Not only did lay women facilitate the historic decision to ordain women, but they regularly invite clergywomen to serve as convention chaplains, speakers, workshop, Bible study or retreat leaders; also, clergywomen learn much from lay women. In the congregation lay women have understood and supported women clergy as they struggled with role expectations and with the demands of juggling professional and home responsibilities. Women tell of hearing the call to ordained service in congregational women's Bible study groups. Local women's groups have eagerly and sacrificially offered moral and financial support to women seminarians. The partnership continues in a myriad of ways.

3. Ann Douglas, *The Feminization of American Culture* (New York: Avon Books, 1977) and Gerda Lerner, *The Majority Finds Its Past.* Oxford: Oxford University Press, 1979.

THE MAGNIFICENT SEVEN

Margaret E. Herz-Lane

WE CALLED OURSELVES the "Magnificent Seven." One can never be quite sure what the church called us, or if it noticed us at all. We were the first African American women ordained into the ministry of Word and Sacrament by the Lutheran Church in America (LCA).

During the early 1980s most of us met on at least two occasions to share both our joys and frustrations with serving in the church. Most, though not all, were pastors to urban congregations. Most, though not all, were associates or assistant pastors and about half in the early 1980s were serving in part-time positions. During those early years receiving a first call to a full-time parish position was for women the exception rather than the rule. Sexism, and for African American women, racism were the two major hurdles yet to overcome. To some who were issued calls the matter of working with senior pastors who were culturally insensitive to African American traditions or who had difficulty working as colleagues with women was an issue.

Erleen Miller was the first African American woman to be ordained in the LCA. Also included in that early group of seven were Gwendolyn King, Cheryl Stewart Pero, Cynthia Schuler (now deceased), Viviane Thomas-Breitfeld, Gwendolyn Johnson-Bond, and me, Margaret Herz-Lane.

I am a parish pastor in an urban setting. Like a number of ordained women, I minister to and advocate for those who often are marginalized by both church and society. This is my story.

79

The place I serve is a small city named Camden. It sits like a diamond on the Delaware River just across from the city of Philadelphia. It is a diamond lost in the rough, a diamond long forgotten in the rush of progress.

People don't come to Camden anymore as much as they pass through it on their way to somewhere else, like "Philly" or the Jersey Shore. It wasn't always that way: There was a time, not so long ago, when all roads led to, not through, Camden, New Jersey. German Lutherans came here in the middle of the 1800s. They organized the *Deutsche Dreifaltigkeitskirche*, now Trinity Lutheran Church, and constructed the main sanctuary building in 1857. Judging from the size and beauty of the building, they were a fairly prosperous group, working people, though, not from a professional class. There were factories and industry to drive the economic engine of the city.

As I walk the neighborhoods of this parish nearly 140 years later, there are still many faces to see, not many heads of gray but strangely hardened young faces, black and brown faces; for this city, now predominantly African American and Puerto Rican American, no longer has the dynamic engines of manufacturing to employ its people. The economic engine today is the death-dealing commerce of crack cocaine and heroin. Drugs have come to shape and frame the lives of the people of this city where banks no longer lend, shopkeepers fear to trade, and the merchants of drugs now rule as princes.

I came to the Camden Lutheran Parish in 1981. It was my first call; I came only weeks after graduating from seminary. It was July and, as in many urban congregations, the parish was in the midst of its summer program. For urban congregations, the summer program is more than an extended vacation Bible school; it is a major form of outreach, a time when the church deliberately goes to the neighborhood surrounding its building and invites the neighborhood to come inside.

At that time, the Camden Lutheran Parish (CLP) was a coalition of four congregations of the former Lutheran Church in America. Ministry in urban coalitions had begun in Philadelphia in the 1960s. The urban coalition, a particular strategy for doing ministry in cities, grew out of the concern to minister to both a congregation and its neighborhood (that is, the parish), the geographic area surrounding the congregation, and was an attempt to marshal resources to do that ministry.

On my internship in Jersey City, New Jersey, I learned first-hand about neighborhood and coalition ministry. While I was an urban person by birth and, as an adult, by preference, the magnitude of urban problems still appeared overwhelming to me. During internship I saw the strength of working together with other pastors and congregations "in coalition" rather than, "going it alone," as an individual pastor and congregation.

The model of "Herr Pastor," an individual who "goes it alone," who operates almost by fiat in a congregation, was at odds with the coalition model of ministry I experienced and grew to appreciate on internship. The coalition model offered an alternative form of ministry and its cooperative rather than competitive flavor appealed to me. However, in the inner city and certainly in the African American community, there is an expectation that pastors will take strong public leadership roles. Thus, the central issue for me as female, black, and pastor was how to provide leadership from a female rather than male perspective. After all, I could never be a "Herr Pastor," either by temperament or by sexual identity.

A coalition, at its best, provides support for both the pastors and congregations as they seek to do ministry in their particular setting. Coalitions offer pastors weekly pericope studies and a support group where they can explore ideas, share concerns, and hold each other accountable for their ministries. In a similar way the coalition offers support to the congregations for lay education, worship events, service projects, and advocating for justice.

The Jersey City coalition had encouraged the development of solid lay leadership, a matter crucial for inner city congregations. In the Camden congregations the majority of the leadership has been female, a reflection of the leadership found in the community as a whole. But, even with solid female leaders, there can be the perception that it is leadership by default, since a strong male presence is often absent in leadership positions.

Since 1981 the Camden parish has included three pastors, a parish worker, a parish musician, and numerous volunteers. In the mid-1970s, the congregations of CLP were among the first in the New Jersey Synod to call a woman as pastor, the Reverend Elizabeth R. Waid, and be served by a female seminary intern, Ruth Drews.

Whenever there was a congregational vacancy in the New Jersey Synod, the assistants to the bishop met with the congregation and call committee in an effort to create a climate accepting of women to the ministry of Word and Sacrament. I think that this combined early exposure of CLP—to women as clergy leaders and to early advocates of women in ministry—helped my acceptance as pastor.

As a black woman I was never discouraged in my intention to serve in an urban, inner city parish. I am aware, however, that my white women counterparts were often cautioned against serving in similar urban settings. In the New Jersey Synod, nevertheless, some of the first women pastors were called to the urban communities of Trenton, Jersey City, and Camden.

I was called as an Urban Resident, an LCA-sponsored program aimed at strengthening and developing the skills of urban pastors. This made it possible for CLP to afford an added pastor. In the urban church, the struggle to obtain both financial and human resources is constant.

Worship is the core reason for our life together; in many urban congregations, particularly those in the Eastern inner cities, weekly Eucharist is fairly common. In Camden, that had been the practice since the mid-1970s when the coalition formed.

As a parish pastor, I have come to see the importance of having a liturgy that is in some way reflective of the cultural and spiritual needs of the people in the pews. As an African American person I have tried to bridge the gaps between my seminary training and the cultural experience of music and worship styles of black and Puerto Rican peoples in this parish.

A source of concern for me, related to the liturgy, has been the problem of illiteracy, particularly as it affects efforts of evangelism and outreach. We Lutherans are people of the book, rather people of many books. Reading for most of our members is not a barrier to worship. However, in the inner city neighborhood where I serve, sixty-five percent of the adults over twenty-five do not have a high school diploma. At the root of this situation, I think, is a problem of illiteracy.

Illiteracy affects all aspects of one's life. A person who can't read, for example, isn't able to assist a child with his or her homework. Employment opportunities are often limited. Self-confidence and a sense of self-worth are often lacking. And illiteracy certainly can affect that person's ability or willingness to be a member of a congregation where literacy is taken for granted.

While urban and church do not automatically equate to poverty, in the case of Camden and CLP they do. This small city of eighty-seven thousand has more than its share of urban problems primarily because of its poverty. North Camden, the neighborhood I serve, has eight thousand residents and a median family income of $11,100. These households are overwhelmingly headed by women, thus women and children who live in poverty are of particular importance to me. As a pastor and a woman I have been most frustrated at the rising rate of teen pregnancy. It is very evident that these early pregnancies will continue to keep young women and their children trapped in poverty with limited options for their futures.

As a result of our particular urban setting, CLP has been involved with the development of programs and projects that offer services to both community residents and congregational members, that is parishioners. The summer program mentioned earlier is one such example. Another, aimed at pregnancy prevention among teenage girls, focuses on self-esteem.

CLP also serves as advocate. A month after my initial arrival in Camden, CLP, Grace Lutheran Church, and residents of North Camden advocated on behalf of the neighborhood when the decision was made by the state of New Jersey to build a six-hundred-bed prison in the neighborhood.

The North Camden neighborhood is one mile square, surrounded on three sides by rivers. In the three-year struggle that followed, we were able to secure money from the state that was used for housing rehabilitation in the area around the new prison. In 1986, the Camden Lutheran Housing Corporation was begun.

Money from that initial effort was used to continue housing rehabilitation in the Grace Church neighborhood. The rehabilitation work on the housing has all been done by local people who have learned building trade skills as a result of this effort. Years later, in 1990, the state of New Jersey attempted to build an additional four-hundred-bed prison in North Camden. This time, the location was to be directly across the street from a junior high school. Both city and suburban church members and residents decried the injustice of this action; the state of New Jersey backed down. In matters of advocacy the community makes few gender distinctions. As a pastor in North Camden I was an integral part of the community discussion and reaction to the proposals by the State of New Jersey, as was expected in my role of pastor and public servant.

Proclamation, service to human need, and advocacy have all been integral to the ministry of Word and sacrament. But the urban ministry of which I have been a part for some thirteen years has changed dramatically. Life in the inner city is now much more difficult for all of us, and especially for the children. The effects of drugs have been particularly devastating to families. Because I am a female pastor I have encouraged the young men of our congregation to work with me in youth programs to model a positive male image for the boys of the church and neighborhood. These youth may have numerous positive examples of women in their lives: mothers, aunts, grandmothers, teachers, and social workers. However, the absence of positive male role models within those same institutions of family and community has had a detrimental effect upon young males.

When young children, usually boys, have access to status and large sums of money with the only requirement being their ability to act as a look-out, school with its daily monotonous grind quickly loses out. With their own money, and in many cases giving money to their parents to help supplement the family income, youngsters in some households have the economic power to dominate and ignore their parents. In other households, where parents are the drug abusers, children are parenting themselves.

In this confusion, the church, regardless of denomination, is the one institution that has not left the inner city. But it is clear that even together we are not able to push back the tide. We are able only to slow down its assault. We exist as a sign to the world that God has not divested from the city. In the lives of the people of this parish, even amidst great tragedy, I have seen that sign.

Luis G., a member of Grace Church, was a sign. In spite of drug abuse by his mother and two of three siblings and his own physical disabilities, Luis, a lifelong resident of North Camden, became an indigenous community leader, known both locally and nationally for his work in community organizing and housing rehabilitation. In the spring of 1994, he proudly completed his associate degree. Just two months later, at age 31, Luis was brutally murdered in his home, a victim of urban violence.

His life and his work live on, however, in the newly rehabilitated houses of the Camden Lutheran Housing Corporation that sit across the street from his church—a sign of new life amidst the devastation.

DO YOU SEE THIS WOMAN?
Barbara K. Lundblad

AFTER MY FIRST YEAR in seminary, I spent the summer working in the parish I had served as youth director five years before. People in the parish knew me from those earlier days, but they did not know me as a preacher. After my first sermon, one of the longtime members, a woman of deep faith who had spent many years in the mission field, told me what she had to do to prepare for my sermon. She said to me: "I told myself, 'Just don't look at her. Listen to the words and don't open your eyes.'" She had never heard a woman preach . . . if she closed her eyes, perhaps she could imagine that the preacher was a man.

"Do you see this woman?" (Luke 7:44).

Jesus posed this question to Simon at a dinner party after an uninvited woman had come into Simon's house to wash Jesus' feet. (Obviously Simon had seen the woman or he wouldn't have been so upset.) But Jesus wanted Simon to *see* her in a new way. "Do you see this woman?" My elderly sister admitted to me that she did open her eyes after I began to preach—and she was still able to listen. We had a lively conversation about the sermon, about our faith, and about women preaching. When I looked out at the congregation on the following summer Sundays, she always had her eyes wide open.

The visible, bodily presence of women in the pulpit changes our notions of who can bear the living word of God. For many people there is an experience of dissonance when they first see and hear a woman preach. The pulpit is the same and the gospel text unchanged—even the alb and stole look familiar, but when a woman stands up to preach things are not the way they used to be. Something shifts inside us that isn't easily explained. Even if a woman were to preach a sermon written by a man, her physical reality would engender a different response.

This dissonance is significant for it raises new questions and challenges old assumptions. It is important to acknowledge this dissonance, even if we seem to have moved beyond it now with many women ordained. In recent years, there have been many discussions about how women's preaching differs from the preaching of men. Journal articles and books point to unique characteristics of women's preaching; dissertations have been written analyzing women's speech patterns in sermons. However, the minute we claim that women tell more stories, someone will surely argue that men too tell stories, especially with the current interest in narrative preaching. If we say that women's preaching style is more emotional, someone will recall a woman who preached without the slightest trace of emotion. Yet, even if we acknowledge the danger of sweeping claims about the uniqueness of women's sermons, one thing at least is true: A woman preaching is a woman preaching. And that is no small thing. It is a visible and audible sign that God has called all people—both women and men—to proclaim the living Word.

"But these words seemed to them an idle tale, and they did not believe them" (Luke 24: 11).

"These words" were the breathless testimony of the women who heard news of resurrection on Easter morning and ran to tell the disciples. "And they did not believe them"—the women or their words. This verse from Luke's Gospel has special meaning for many women, ordained and lay. Women identify with this gospel text in a way men do not and this has implications for women's preaching. Though both women and men are called to preach the resurrection gospel, women stand in a different place and hear from a different vantage point. Women have often stood at the edge of the crowd, not counted in the numbering at Sinai nor in the arithmetic of those five thousand men fed by Jesus on the hillside. Women have brought their egg money and mission offerings to church, but could not vote at church meetings. Women have experienced their words dismissed as idle tales, only to see them picked up later by a man on the board and voted into action.

Women who preach come to the scripture text and the pulpit standing in a place that is different from the place of their brothers. This affects how women hear the biblical texts, how they hear the texts of the community, and how they bring the two together in preaching.

Women preachers have paid close attention to biblical stories of women, not only laughing with Sarah, but also weeping in anguish with Hagar. There is a point of deep identification between women preachers and women of the biblical stories. Why did Ruth leave home and why did Orpah stay in the familiar place? Why is Bathsheba always remembered as "Uriah's wife?" In partnership with feminist biblical scholars, women preachers have given voice to their silenced sisters raped, abused, and misused within the pages of Scripture. Who will remember the concubine abused and dismembered (Judges 19)? In the words of Phyllis Trible, "Where are the words that speak to her heart?"[1]

Women have also pushed against the binding of the lectionary itself. They have wondered: Why isn't the story of the hemorrhaging woman ever read in the three-year cycle? Why don't we let her interrupt the story of Jairus's daughter even as she interrupted Jesus? In their preaching, women have sought out the stories that never made it into the lectionary, the lost coins of our biblical tradition. Where are the courageous Hebrew midwives Shiphrah and Puah (Exodus 1:15-22)? Or the stubborn Shunammite woman who insisted that Elisha himself come down from the mountain to raise her little boy from death (2 Kings 4:18-37)?

This doesn't mean that women never preach about Moses or Peter (or that men never preach about Hannah or Mary). It does mean that stories long neglected have been cherished and revitalized in the preaching of women. While the overwhelming

BARBARA K. LUNDBLAD

weight of the biblical tradition remains masculine, this renewed attention to the stories of women has brought a needed corrective—and a deeply important theological affirmation that male and female are created in the image of God.

This attentiveness to women's stories goes beyond the pages of the Bible. Standing with the women dismissed on Easter morning, women preachers have leaned forward, listening for the unspoken stories of their sisters this side of Scripture. Silence has been broken and women's experience is no longer discounted. Words never uttered before—incest, battering, sexual abuse—have been spoken aloud in the pulpit. Women's lives are taken seriously. A lay woman told me some years ago, "I feel safe when women preach." She went on to say that she has sometimes been disappointed, but she begins with the presumption of safety: My life will be honored. I will not be demeaned nor trivialized.

At times, this means that feminist preachers have found it necessary to preach against the text, or at least against the traditional interpretation of the text. If a text oppresses women, how can it be gospel? How does a woman who has spent a lifetime giving herself up for others hear Jesus' call to lose her life? How does an abused woman hear Jesus' words about bearing the cross—especially if a pastor has told her that this abuse is the cross she has to bear to keep her marriage intact? In her recent book *She Who Is*, theologian Elizabeth Johnson urges us to uphold the least among our sisters: "For me the goal of feminist religious discourse pivots in its fullness around the flourishing of poor women of color in violent situations."[2] We Lutherans have been trained to read all of Scripture through the prism of the gospel principle of justification by grace through faith. Feminist pastors and scholars also urge us to see that Scripture must be interpreted with women's well-being in mind—or how can the gospel in its fullness be heard?

"But she answered him, 'Sir, even the dogs under the table eat the children's crumbs' " (Mark 7:28).

These are the words of the feisty Syrophonecian woman who begged Jesus to heal her daughter. She took Jesus' name-calling in stride, picking up his words and throwing them back to claim her place at the table. She is a crafty woman, crafty as Rachel who hid her father's household gods beneath her and said, "I cannot rise before you, for the way of women is upon me" (Genesis 31:35). What can be said about the *craftiness* of women preachers?

Though there are pitfalls in claiming too much, there are signs that women's preaching is indeed different from men's. It is no accident that one of the first books published about women and preaching was *Weaving the Sermon* by Christine Smith.[3] Weaving is a word many women use to describe the preaching craft. The biblical story is woven together with stories from the congregation and community. These stories move in and around each other, and unlikely colors are set side by side to create surprising new patterns. It may not be possible to outline such a sermon for it doesn't move from point A to point B in neat linear fashion.

Quilting is another metaphor women choose for their preaching—even though homiletics textbooks written in years past describe "ladder sermons" or speak about strong foundations and building blocks. Though I have never made a quilt myself, I find the image compelling—taking what is old, used, faded, and discarded and fashioning it into something new, beautiful, and useful.

The fiftieth anniversary of the Protestant Hour, a weekly radio ministry of the Evangelical Lutheran Church in America, was celebrated with a special series entitled "The Past Speaks to the Present." Pastor John Vannorsdall and I were partnered in the series: His was a sermon from 1983 and my sermon from twelve years later. Both of us focused on the same biblical text. During the program the two of us conversed on the air about how we had each approached the text. Our sermons were indeed very different. I had used an image from a poem as a metaphor for Jesus' prayer that the disciples might be one (John 17:11):

BARBARA K. LUNDBLAD

Dear Lord, lest we all be somewhere else, patch this work. Quilt us together, feather-stitching piece by piece our tag-ends of living, our individual scraps of love.[4]

When we talked together, Vannersdoll said, "It would never have entered my head to use an image of quilting."

Indeed, it is probably true that women carry in their heads images that are not in men's heads. It is not a matter of better or worse, simply different. Still, something is missing when only images of men's work or sports are heard from the pulpit. In their preaching women have not only brought images from their own life experience, they have introduced the writings of women poets and storytellers, theologians, and foremothers in the faith.

And women's sermons have spun out new ways of speaking about God. Though this is not true of all women who preach, it has become critically important to many, both preachers and hearers. Again, I turn to Elizabeth Johnson:

> "The mystery of God transcends all images but can be spo-ken about equally well and poorly in concepts taken from male or female reality. . . . Only if the full reality of women as well as men enters into the symbolization of God . . . can the idolatrous fixation on one image be broken."[5]

We cannot change Scripture so that God is Mother rather than Father. We cannot rewrite the historic creeds using female lan-guage. Though such formulations might indeed proclaim fuller truth about God, they would not be the historic creeds tying us to the church throughout time and space. Preaching, however, offers rich possibilities for speaking of God in ways that open us to female images while changes in the language of liturgy and prayer may still be too jarring.

The preacher reads and rereads the text. She sees and hears. She remembers and discovers: The Hebrew words for *womb* and *mercy* come from the same root; they are organically connected. How can she speak of this God, this merciful, womb-of-a-God? Parables and images, narratives and songs emerge in the heart and mind of the preacher. The sermon gently nudges hearers to see God embracing her children. The preacher begins with small stories set side by side—like the pairing in Luke's Gospel of the shepherd searching for one lamb alongside the woman searching for one lost coin. Over time the images grow and fill more space. And the face of God that shines upon us in the Benediction begins to reflect the image of women as well as men.

And that, sisters and brothers, is no small thing.

Notes

1. Phyllis Trible, *Texts of Terror: Literary-Feminist Readings of Biblical Narratives* (Philadelphia: Fortress Press, 1984), p. 9.

2. Elizabeth Johnson, *She Who Is: The Mystery of God in Feminist Theological Discourse* (New York: Crossroad Publishing Company, 1993), p. 11.

3. Christine M. Smith, *Weaving the Sermon: Preaching in a Feminist Perspective*, (Louisville, Ky.: Westminster/John Knox, 1989).

4. Jane Wilson Joyce, "Crazy Quilt," in *Cries of the Spirit*, ed. Marilyn Sewell (Boston: Beacon Press, 1991), p. 135.

5. Elizabeth Johnson, *She Who Is: The Mystery of God in Feminist Theological Discourse* (New York: Crossroad Publishing Company, 1993), p. 56.

SISTERS WHO BEAR THE WORD
Mary E. F. Albing

FIVE YEARS BEFORE my ordination, and a lifetime away on the other side of the globe, I met Blandine Aimee, a young Malagasy woman. My husband was completing his pastoral internship. I was helping to organize a nurse's station for students, teaching English, sorting out financial records, and learning about missionary life.

Blandine was studying church history, biblical languages, and systematics with her future husband and several others who attended a regional seminary. She taught us Malagasy and helped us to understand the culture. But more than that, in that hot desert of southern Madagascar she offered us the refreshment of her friendship.

Born a bishop's daughter, she was an exceptionally gifted student. Now she is a bishop's wife at least as capable as her husband. She cannot be a pastor, since the Malagasy Lutheran church does not ordain women. Perhaps she will never be ordained. Though it is no small thing—this privilege that she is denied—she preaches, teaches, and ministers all the same. She faithfully bears the Word in the heat and poverty of a small village in Madagascar.

On December 18, 1988, I was ordained into the holy ministry of Word and sacrament. It was the Fourth Sunday in Advent and the Gospel for the day was the Magnificat. The preacher, my mentor Sheldon Tostengard, drew comparisons between me and Mary the mother of our Lord, the first woman to bear the Word.

"While from our perspective these two Marys don't seem much alike, they are in some ways very similar, because they are drawn together by the blessing of the baby Jesus who has become for us the Word of God. Just as Mary of old, while unworthy, was entrusted with a great task, so also is this Mary about to be ordained about to undertake a great work. And just as Mary of old has been sustained in the life of the church by her relationship with Jesus, so also will this new pastor be sustained by that living Word."[1]

That day, with the weight of the hands laid on my head, the prayers and the promises that sent me into my first call, I keenly felt the responsibility of bearing the Word. I went away from that service and into my work sustained by the image of bearing the Word, caring for it like a child in the womb, as Mary did, and being blessed by it.

At the same time, I realized, that unlike Mary, I did not bear the Word alone. Many women, like Blandine, share that holy work. Bertha is another. As a member of the congregation Bertha faithfully carries the elements for Holy Communion down the stairs to Friday Fellowship, a service intended for the older members of the congregation. She carefully prepares the altar for worship, then helps prepare for the lunch that follows. She visits with each person who is present. She bears Jesus in the Lord's Supper and in her presence to those who come.

Bertha has been bearing the Word all her life. This task of bearing the Word is her responsibility and mine, together, in this congregation. And I am grateful to her.

She holds me responsible in the most gentle way to the gospel. Bertha keeps me steadfast in my work by asking questions and telling me who needs Communion. She allows me to join in her work and life, and to make a difference with her. She supports me. Together we point to the Savior. Bertha and I work together in the gospel, in fun, in respect, in love for one another. If I were not ordained, perhaps I could be like Bertha.

MARY E. F. ALBING

I am aware that I serve the church with Bertha and Blandine. The same church that nurtures them, and that they serve, has shaped and formed me. In my childhood and youth, I was its student and relied on the direction of the Christian community. As a young adult I offered my gifts and relied on the love of the same community. Finally, grown and ordained, I lead and minister and still rely on my community for love and direction and support. In most ways, my work in the church is simply understood, since I've been a part of it all my life, just as Bertha and Blandine have been a part of it all their lives.

In struggling for the words to describe myself and my vocation, I asked a colleague, a church professional who had worked with many pastors, how it was different to work with a woman pastor. She said without hesitation, "You encourage us." Then she thought a moment and added, "But not only that, you pitch right in and help us." It occurred to me that my women friends and colleagues who are ordained interact with their congregations in much the same way. They encourage the laity, but more than that, they work beside and among them.

By December 18, 1988, the privilege of ordination that had been so hard fought for was already taken for granted by many. I admit that I did not worry that particular day about my ministry's effect or my own acceptance. It was a calling. It was the right thing to do.

On that day, my mentor continued:

"Soon this Mary about to be ordained will have special reason for joy. For she will have acknowledged and she will have taken upon herself a great calling—that of the holy ministry. Soon she will stand in that noble company of pastors who have hurried the word of the resurrection to the side of the dying, who have preached hope when there is often only despair. Soon she will stand among that noble company of pastors who have made the sign of the cross on the brow and the breast of millions of grimacing children. Soon this woman will become a part of the noble company of preachers and her spirit will rejoice because the Word that summons her, that Word who is our Lord Jesus will shape and mold her ministry and her life. Just as Elizabeth's babe leaped in praise of Mary, and just as Mary sang her song in praise of God, so shall the Word that is Jesus be the praise that goes up from our Mary's ministry and that Word will be for her a precious treasure."[2]

Women now stand alongside men in a "noble company" and do what comes most naturally because of their gifts and the call of God who wishes to bless and save. But if ordained ministry were taken away from me for some reason, I would hope to minister as Bertha and Blandine and many have through the ages.

In the daily serving, in pointing towards God's presence, in valuing what sometimes seems to be valueless, in enacting and imitating God's ways, in hoping against hopelessness, I wish simply to take my place alongside other faithful ministers of all times and places. Women have, after all, always been important to the life of the church, though unrecognized and even unnamed. The women at the tomb did not know that centuries later women would cling to their story to prove that God wanted them to declare the hope of the resurrection. And how could the woman at the well, or the woman who anointed Jesus, those who were despised, dream that their encounters with Christ could be cherished by other women who ministered to others so many years later? Unspoken, unsung, but ministers all the same, women have always served, have always been bearing the Word together. I take comfort in knowing that my call to the holy ministry, while a great privilege, is shared by all these women.

One day I stood in the small church kitchen visiting with the women who were busy cleaning up after Friday Fellowship lunch. I had presided over worship and they were marvelling about how a woman preacher fit in. Bertha said, "It seems like you've always been here." And so it does.

Notes

1. From ordination sermon delivered December 18, 1988.
2. *Ibid.*

NEW PATTERNS FOR MINISTRY
Carolyn Mercedes Mowchan

OUR PARISH ASSISTANT commented to me recently that my husband and I seem to work smoothly together as a team. I could only smile and give thanks privately for the many lessons we've learned in the past twelve years as a clergy couple.

Women entering the seminary to prepare for ministry brought about inevitable changes on campus, one of them being romance. Clergy couples made up about six percent of the total rostered clergy in the Evangelical Lutheran Church in America (ELCA) in 1994.[1] Clergy couples share with clergywomen the task of finding and creating new patterns for ministry. We raise issues for the seminary, for bishops, and for congregations. Some of the issues raised are: learning to build and separate professional and private relationships, modeling shared power, and creatively developing multiple staff calls and job descriptions. We also bring surprising and unexpected gifts to the church.

Clergy couples often seek each other out to ask, "How's it going?" We know instinctively that there are common threads to the task that we share in our journey to shape ministry together. Of course, there are as many varieties in the stories we could all tell as there are differences in individual marriages. I write of my own story with other voices in my ears. Like the story of all humanity, the voices speak of great joy and of great burdens.

One of the questions I am often asked by men is, "Who's the boss?" The question is real. It is usually followed by the comment, "My wife and I could never work together in the same office. How do you manage it?" Women tend to ask about whether the work relationship strains the marriage relationship. They ask questions like, "When do you get away from each other?" Their questions acknowledge the need for privacy. Men seem more concerned with the balance of power.

When clergy couples are perceived as a risk it is more than a matter of the risk of the unknown. The risk, when it is articulated, is the knowledge that most marriages are not based on a model of equitable power. The assumption is that the power struggles within a marriage relationship would be increased to unwieldy proportions if they were also carried into the workplace. This assumption is a barrier that clergy couples often face early in their career.

We first faced such assumptions at the seminary. Our dream as a couple was always one of team ministry. We met and married during our seminary years and so faced the task of simultaneously creating both a stable marriage and a workable professional relationship. These are separate tasks, requiring more emotional honesty than some couples are ready for. The complexity of the task was perhaps more clear to our friends than to us.

When couples announce during their seminary years that they would like to work together, they are often asked questions about their self-esteem and their ability to set boundaries for themselves and for the congregation. I was asked, "Can you really be your own person while working with your husband?" Questions of this sort raise any number of issues, some beyond the scope of seminary class work and so the seminary hesitates to encourage couples to pursue joint ministry.

In an effort to protect the couple and the supervising pastor from struggles during their internship experience, the seminary discourages married students from interning in the same parish. This merely postpones unresolved issues to a future time. It means, at best, that couples seeking a joint call after graduation don't know yet whether they can work together comfortably or not.

I asked the seminary to allow me to do my internship in the congregation where my husband, Will, was the associate pastor. The senior pastor agreed to be my supervisor and was willing to argue in support of our request. That argument was rather intense and unpleasant.

Our goal was to open our relationship to the assistance of the senior pastor in an effort to help us build a solid clergy couple ministry. We argued that it would be better to deal with issues of competition, control, and communication during a year when we had helpful resources available to us than to deal with these issues alone in a call situation.

We were able to convince the seminary that it was a good idea. Unfortunately it didn't work. None of us were prepared for issues that triangles can create. We often felt that as a couple we were aligned against the senior pastor. The senior pastor wasn't comfortable with the dynamics created by a married couple and by his role as mediator, colleague, and supervisor. After a few awkward attempts as a staff of three, we lived out the duration of our staff time together in a pained silence.

We had been told, "couples really need to do their homework before they try to work together." We hadn't. I thought that since we had divided our household responsibilities in untraditional ways, we clearly understood balancing power. But the deeper issues go beyond the fact that Will does all the cooking at our house.

We had not asked ourselves some very basic questions such as: How do we disagree? When we disagree, and we will, can we manage conflict in a way that doesn't discredit our faith and ministry? How do we understand the balance of power in our relationship? Are we prepared for issues of competition? Are we threatened by our differences or do they give us strength we can rely on? Where do we go for support when we need to talk, especially when our partner may be "talked out" at any given time?

Self-esteem comes into play in subtle ways. If we are not clearly defined as separate persons within our own minds, then the divisions or boundaries between us may be nebulous. Can either one of us let the other make his or her own mistakes without feeling responsible? In other words, can he and I give each other the professional distance and freedom that is needed in any healthy staff situation? The issue here is control.

Looking back, my primary stress in our early years of marriage and ministry together was the process of trying to re-create my husband in my own image. I wanted him to read my thoughts, speak my language and probably, if I'm honest, do ministry the way I do ministry. I saw his maleness as something that needed to be tempered by my femaleness. This is a nice way of saying I was pretty arrogant. It is also a subtle way of saying I wanted the power to win battles, have the last word, and shape our ministry. Hindsight is wonderful. But the wisdom was expensive.

When it was time to consider calls, Will and I decided that we wanted some combination of full and part-time.[2] Full-time calls usually mean more than full-time, and knowing that, we were hesitant to seek two full-time positions. We wanted to manage parenting, marriage, and ministry without becoming the stereotypical burned-out pastors.

Part-time ministry raises possibilities and difficulties for the church. For those medium-sized congregations that need more than one full-time pastor but can't afford or don't yet need two full-time pastors, clergy couples are often the perfect solution for their needs. For very small parishes yoked by size and financial need, a clergy couple can be called to share one multi-parish call, and yet each can still have her or his own congregation.

Couples who want other people to set limits for them find that "part-time" usually means full-time with a part-time salary. Couples who have clearly stated that the health of their family is a priority, and so put limits on their time, may meet with resistance from those who are still working with other models of ministry. Pastors seeking part-time positions, as a couple or individually, can expect that initial placement may be a slow process, and mobility is more difficult.

Will and I waited more than a year for an interview both times we sought placement. Although it wasn't our first preference, our first call was not together. I served two very small churches and Will served a third, larger one. My two churches were so far out in the country I asked the all-male call committee

CAROLYN MERCEDES MOWCHAN

if I would be safe as a woman alone keeping office hours. Members of the committee replied with puzzled sincerity, "We haven't seen bear on the property for many years."

We found that the isolation from our friends and roots, three churches, two small children, and the stresses of antagonistic congregations, not to mention the need for mission and evangelism tools we didn't feel that we possessed, put great strain on our relationship. The issues we had not dealt with on internship surfaced in crisis proportions.

We finally did our homework. With the help of counseling, prayer, the support of friends and our bishop, and the painfully slow process of reconciliation and forgiveness, we were once again able to minister together. Out of that experience we resolved to seek a call where we could work together and have a church home for our family.

I can now honestly say that when people see a husband and wife working together, bringing separate gifts and perspectives to ministry, sharing faith, balancing power, and working hard to create a Christian environment for their children to thrive in, it is a strong witness to the power of God and an important model for other families. It certainly takes God's help to make this possible.

As I write this, we have been in our current parish for more than a year. Our call is one-and-a-half time in one congregation. I work nine months at three-quarter time. Our family is thriving, our parish is thriving, and ministry is equally a gift and a joy for both of us. Thanks be to God.

Notes

1. Martin H. Smith, interview by author, November 19, 1994, phone conversation. These numbers are approximate and based on 1994 figures from the ELCA Department for Research and Evaluation leadership files.

2. *Ibid.* Smith, a research associate with the ELCA Department for Research and Evaluation, says that for nearly forty-four percent of senior pastors, full-time calls means working sixty-plus hours per week.

NOT BOUND BY PATTERNS OR TRADITIONS: BEING A FIRST

Cynthia Ganzkow-Wold

ON MARCH 1, 1992, I began a call as senior pastor of St. Luke's Lutheran Church in Middleton, Wisconsin. St. Luke's is a congregation of more than two thousand members located in the Evangelical Lutheran Church in America (ELCA) South Central Synod of Wisconsin. It was soon to embark on a multimillion dollar building project, to select a new twelve-person pastoral and support staff, and to transform the congregation into a center for worship and mission.

Even though in 1977 I was the first clergywoman in the South Dakota District of the American Lutheran Church (ALC) (and years later one of the first females in the Evangelical Lutheran Church [ELCA] to accept a senior pastorate call to a large congregation) it seemed like the result of a natural progression in my professional ministry. Prior to my present position, I spent nine years in South Dakota, in a two-point rural parish and as an associate in a large parish, followed by a six-year stint as a campus pastor at the University of Wisconsin—Madison, with the final two years as the director of campus ministry. When I accepted the call as senior pastor of St. Luke's, my fifteen years of pastoral ministry had successfully intertwined my pastoral identity with my professional skills.

While being a woman is an important aspect of my pastoral identity and pastoral work, it is not ultimately the defining factor in determining the direction of my ministry. Since my first days at Luther Seminary in St. Paul, Minnesota in 1973, to my present senior pastorate in 1995, I have always strongly believed that the Spirit of God has called, enlightened, and sanctified me in my Christian faith and in my pastoral ministry. This sense of call, first experienced in my college days at the University of Minnesota (in the early 1970s), has been the guiding factor in leading me through eighteen years of ordained ministry. The work of God's Spirit has also been a source of strength and hope to me during challenging and difficult moments as a pastor and, more specifically, as an ordained woman in the church.

It seems as if much of what I have experienced over the years has been a "first." I was the first woman assigned to the South Dakota District of the ALC, the first female pastor in both of my initial pastorates, the first female director of a multi-pastoral campus ministry staff, and now the first woman in ordained ministry to lead a large congregation in our synod.

On the one hand, being a first gave me the freedom to develop a ministry that has not yet been bound by patterns or traditions introduced by another Lutheran clergywoman. As a first I was able to develop a previously undefined role for myself, one that built on my strengths. With that came a sense of accomplishment that was both gratifying and satisfying. But, on the other hand, being a first meant that there were few, if any, female role models or colleagues with whom I could fully identify or who were able to speak from experience. I was seen as an anomaly. This was a unique experience for me, one that set me apart from my male colleagues who serve large parishes, and one that ultimately found me on my own. Once, for example, I attended a conference for senior pastors of large ELCA congregations with more than one hundred in attendance. I was a unique but noticeable participant. I could not help but feel like an intruder and often sensed that I was expected to represent all women who are clergy.

I do feel the increased burdens of scrutiny that accompany being a first, but I would consider it an honor if my being one of the first female senior pastors of the ELCA might help open doors for other competent and faithful ordained women to be considered for positions of senior pastorates in the church.

I have been asked if a glass ceiling exists in the church and if, in fact, ordained women are being denied positions of leadership. Change in the church does not come easily. Traditions die hard, but the growing numbers of ordained women will enable the church to assess pastoral faithfulness and skills on the basis of characteristics that include gender as a gift and a strength rather than as a liability or an aberration.

The set of gifts that I bring to the position of senior pastor are a reflection of the many gifts brought by women to the ministry of Word and sacrament, only one of which is gender. It would be foolish to separate gender as an issue in and of itself, but my experiences as a woman, my personal, pastoral and theological understandings as a female, and my varied ministry experiences as a woman ordained into the ministry of the church have resulted in a set of gifts that remain unique to the church.

The development and progression of my ministry as a pastor has been aided by my deep belief in the importance of mentors and partners in the faith and in daily ministry. Professors, colleagues, friends, family, parishioners, students, and others along the way have been important teachers and mentors in the deepening of my understandings of Christianity, Lutheranism, ministry, and the priesthood of all believers. In addition, I would cite the strong support of my bishop, who has been a source of great strength and encouragement.

I also place a strong emphasis on partnership in pastoral ministry, and have valued the opportunities to work with colleagues, both women and men, who have joined together in our efforts to proclaim the gospel of Jesus Christ. The same can be said for the people I serve, who allow me not only to minister to them but who, in many ways, minister to me. Without these ongoing relationships, ministry would not be possible. For in the end, pastoral ministry is not about who or what I am or we are, but pastoral ministry is about the Holy One we serve.

WOMEN IN CHURCHWIDE AND SEMINARY MINISTRY

Margaret A. Krych

TOWARD THE END of 1972 I met with Dr. Kent Gilbert, executive director of the Lutheran Church in America's Division for Parish Services (DPS) and accepted a position as editor for early elementary resources. Soon after, I received a call to that position and was ordained in the Lutheran Church in America (LCA) in March, 1973.

ON CHURCHWIDE STAFF

In a sense, I was one of the lucky ones—an ordained woman who did not have to face some of the difficulties experienced by my sister pastors who were pioneers in ministry in congregations. The DPS that began operating in September of 1972 already had a good number of lay women on staff, and I as the first ordained woman staff person joined the editorial team with a sense of support and encouragement.[1] I found DPS to be an exciting and challenging opportunity for ministry. I learned a great deal about the national church while producing educational resources for use in congregations. There were opportunities to relate to synods and also to other Lutheran bodies. DPS was supportive of women's issues and women in ministry. While I was there the LCA drew up guidelines for inclusive language in resources and editors worked hard to ensure that educational resources were inclusive in content and in art.

In those years, I watched with joy the successes of women pastors and with sadness their struggles in the parish. Before coming to the United States to do graduate studies in 1970, I was one of the first women to serve in ordained ministry in the Methodist Church in Australia. Having already discovered in seminary the ecumenical treasure that Lutheran theology brings to the whole church, and having planned at Princeton Theological Seminary to write a doctoral dissertation on a Lutheran theologian, it was not long before I began to study seriously the Lutheran Confessions and to worship with a Lutheran congregation in the U.S. This eventually led to a request for membership and later ordination in the LCA. But my memories of Australian ministry were fresh. I knew firsthand the fears of and prejudice towards female pastors by church members and by the community at large.

Pioneers experience loneliness and frustration as they take curiosity, questioning, and rejection along with welcoming and acceptance in parish ministry. So, while I served on the national staff of the LCA, I empathized with my sisters in parish ministry in the Lutheran church and with those who were training in seminaries. I felt as if I were watching a familiar scenario, albeit on a different continent and in a different denomination. Many congregations in the United States had prejudices and fears of the unknown similar to those in my homeland. I felt a responsibility to preach and preside whenever possible so that congregations that might otherwise not see and hear a woman pastor would do so. Dr. Edwin Ehlers, then president of the New Jersey Synod, was supportive of women in ministry and the synod office was always ready to encourage women to be in the pulpit.

Ironically, in the late seventies, institutions that actually wanted to support women were not always helpful. On one occasion, I received a letter from a university in another part of the country inviting me to consider a faculty position. The letter indicated that the institution really did not care what I taught or what field I was in—just that it needed a woman on faculty and that any woman pursuing or holding a Ph.D. would do. I felt insulted and disturbed by this approach to hiring women in academia (and told them so). It was my first warning that people

MARGARET A. KRYCH

might want me for my gender and not because of any careful scholarship I might have done. I wasn't too sure whether outright prejudice against women wasn't easier to take than condescending tokenism.

CALL FOR WOMEN FACULTY

In 1977, I left DPS to accept a call to The Lutheran Theological Seminary at Philadelphia (which did care what field I was in and what study I had done). The seminary was concerned that there were no women on faculty. At that time there were far fewer women students than there are today, but those who were there needed role models of ordained women in faculty positions. Although ordination of women had been approved in 1970, the numbers of women entering seminary grew gradually, and it would be years before the percentage of women in the student body would be close to half, as it is today. Many women students experienced prejudice or were received with suspicion in field education and internship. Those who had negative experiences needed to reflect on them with faculty members. And those who had positive experiences needed encouragement and guidance as they set out in ministry.

Teaching was and is a most rewarding form of ministry and I loved the faculty position from the beginning. There were many demands on the time of a woman faculty member and all were important. In addition to preparing for class and teaching, we were counseling women students or making ourselves available to those wanting to talk and unload. Local parishes would phone with questions about interviewing a woman as pastor or inviting a woman to preach. These parishes needed reassurance, and often a listening ear as they struggled with a move they knew they should make, yet were afraid to take. Committees rightly felt the need for women to be represented and called on faculty members to fill many roles. Of course, there were also responsibilities of completing a dissertation, and writing and publishing. Inevitably, those of us who were early women members of faculties felt that we had to "do it all" simply because there were still so few of us and because we felt that so much rested on giving good female leadership in this time of new opportunity for women in the church.

Gradually, as more women joined faculties, the novelty began to wear off and the burden of engagements lessened somewhat, although the burden is still often disproportionate to that of male faculty members simply because there are not yet enough women teaching in seminaries. However, since 1970 when there were no women with faculty rank in Lutheran seminaries, I have seen genuine efforts over the years to attract female faculty members. Seminaries have advertised positions widely to make women aware of openings and have encouraged women to apply for positions. More recently, the Evangelical Lutheran Church in America (ELCA) Division for Ministry has regularly kept and distributed an updated list of women in graduate programs who may be interested in receiving information concerning ELCA seminary, college and university teaching positions. There appears to be a desire to bring over time a male-female balance to faculties that will reflect more closely the ratio in student bodies. In search processes, most seminaries, all qualifications being judged equal, will give preference to women or persons of color. As I write, there are thirty-eight women (lay and ordained, Lutheran and non-Lutheran) who have faculty rank in ELCA seminaries. And as early as 1978, the first woman (Faith Burgess) was appointed as academic dean of a Lutheran seminary (The Lutheran Theological Seminary at Philadelphia).

While it will take still more time before there is significant representation of women faculty and administrators in our ELCA seminaries, I rejoice that I serve on a faculty that has four women (lay and ordained, Lutheran and Presbyterian) two of whom are in tenure-track positions. With more women in graduate programs in divinity, there should be a greater proportion of women on seminary faculties across the United States.[2]

EARLY YEARS IN MINISTRY

Women often find it difficult to know which negative reactions to their ministry are deserved critiques of their work and which are due solely to prejudice against women in ministry. They may often blame themselves for the former when in fact it is the latter.

MARGARET A. KRYCH

In those early years I found it hard to judge which reactions to my ministry were due to my being female and which reactions might be due to the fact that I had previously been a Methodist pastor and that I had been born and bred in another country.

One of the greatest problems that all of us had to bear was to respond to innumerable requests to belong to committees, to preach, to speak. This burden was especially felt by those on national staff and seminaries. Since we were not tied to a weekly congregational schedule, we felt the responsibility to represent women, to allow the voice of women to be heard, to enable congregations and groups to experience ministry from women firsthand. But, because there were so few of us, the demands were incredible. And they were not only for preaching and speaking. Synodical examining committees needed ordained women. National church committees needed ordained women. Boards and task forces needed ordained women. And there just didn't seem enough of us to go around. Yet it was imperative that the church's needs be met. So most of us took on far too many responsibilities and spread ourselves too thin.

Added to this was the fact that I was a pastor's wife and had two children, born in 1973 and 1981. So I was trying to juggle being a pastor's spouse and a parent along with my ministry. Of course, congregations were used to pastor's spouses working. But they weren't used to them being ministers. I recall a pulpit committee coming to hear my husband preach while I was supplying in another congregation. I returned after the service to my husband's congregation to greet the committee at the coffee hour and found them politely puzzled as to my absence during the service and curious as to how often this might occur should my husband become their pastor.

If I had an image of those early years in ministry, it would be one of running: to the sitter, to work, to the airport, to meetings, to committees, to preaching engagements, to the store. Always, go, go. . . .

Would I do it again? Of course. The call to service does not promise comfort and an easy life. But the struggles only serve to highlight the joy and delight that ministry brings. Preaching and celebrating the sacraments, teaching and sharing the good news, serving the church of Jesus Christ—these are the what ministry is about. We thank God for twenty-five years of women in ordained ministry, and we look with hope and confidence to the work of the Spirit through women in the decades ahead.

Notes

1. "Male dominance in churchwide staff positions was a serious problem, with only 20 out of 169 professional level places held by women in 1978, and 11 of those were in the Division for Parish Services. One small breakthrough occurred . . . when Margaret Krych became the first ordained woman staff person, but by the end of the decade, there still was only one." W. Kent Gilbert, *Commitment to Unity* (Philadelphia, Fortress Press, 1988), p. 299.

2. Phyllis Anderson, "Lutheran Women in Theological Studies," *Lutheran Women in Ordained Ministry 1970-1995: Reflections and Perspectives* (Minneapolis: Augsburg Books), pp. 129-136.

WOMEN OF COLOR AND THE TWENTY-FIFTH ANNIVERSARY OF THE ORDINATION OF WOMEN IN THE LUTHERAN CHURCH

Cheryl Stewart Pero

IT WAS THE SPRING of 1972 and I was nearing the end of my junior year at Wellesley College. I was a twenty-year-old from the Bronx, a member of St. Paul's Evangelical Lutheran Church of Tremont, a congregation of The Lutheran Church–Missouri Synod (LCMS), a fairly recent graduate of Our Saviour Lutheran High School, and a young West Indian/African American woman. I was the first family member of my generation to go to college. My majors were classical civilization and child psychology. I was prepared also to become a primary educator though I did not want to become either a teacher or a deaconess, the only two church vocations that were open to women. I had long ago put away my childhood fantasies of becoming a doctor or a lawyer. What was I going to do after graduation?

Because my social life revolved around church, it was only natural while at college to become involved with campus ministry. The campus pastor was the Reverend Paul Santmire, of the Lutheran Church in America (LCA). It was to Santmire that I found myself confiding one day: my fears and anxieties, my insecurities and lack of options, my identity struggles and identification issues, my indecision. It was he who first asked me if I had ever thought about the ministry as a vocation. Growing up in the LCMS meant that I had never considered being a pastor as a vocational option. Nevertheless in the fall of 1972, my senior year, I had been accepted at Andover Newton Theological School (ANTS) in Newton Center, Massachusetts. I had decided to enroll, not planning on ordained ministry, but because I felt that wherever I went from there, I would bring with me some basic theological training as well as a better understanding of whose I was and what I was about.

It was also during these formative college and seminary years, while living near the explosive city of Boston, that I began to realize the breadth of institutional racism and how the sin of racism permeates our entire society, including the church. The city of Boston was my classroom. Between the conflict over Boston public school desegregation and the racial conflicts that often erupted in South and East Boston, the city proved to be the best crucible for my training. Since those days I have always worked actively in the area of anti-racist education and training.

In the spring of 1977, during my last semester at ANTS, I took a leave of absence to study at Lutheran School of Theology at Chicago (LSTC). I spent the 1977 calendar year in Chicago fulfilling the Lutheran seminary year requirement, beginning work on a Master of Theology in Church and Society (a degree I received in 1981), and becoming a member of the LCA.

Being one of the few women of color in the Lutheran church who, by 1977, had completed basic theological training, I received an offer to join the staff of the LCA in New York. I remember with fondness Reverend Kenneth Senft, Executive Director of the Division for Ministry in North America (DMNA), engaging me in a number of discussions about the ordination of women and my impatience with the slowness of change in the church. Although we ultimately resolved nothing, I felt that someone was finally listening to and hearing the concerns of women.

Once my eyes were opened to the possibility of ordained ministry, and after various members of my ethnic/racial community encouraged me to become a pastor, I never gave up on my goal of seeking ordination. I left my position at DMNA in mid-1979 to fulfill my internship year in Gary, Indiana. I was ordained on May 18th, 1980, by the Illinois Synod of the LCA, under the leadership of Bishop Paul E. Erickson. I was the second African American woman to be ordained in the history of American Lutheranism.[1]

My first call was to serve as the associate pastor of Resurrection Lutheran Church, a European American congregation on the north side of Chicago. During these years a number of my European American sisters were ordained and called to serve in neighboring congregations. Very seldom did support relationships develop between us, despite the fact that most of us were in team ministries, because we were dealing with very different issues in our respective ministry settings. I was focused on defending my culture, my gender, and my ministry in a hostile context while my sisters focused on establishing themselves as equal partners with their European American male colleagues in less hostile contexts.

When the fifteenth anniversary celebration of the ordination of women was being planned, I was certain that the Lutheran judicatories would chose to herald the ordinations of Hispanic and African American women as major milestones in the celebration of the ordination of all women. Many women of color had been ordained during the five-year interim between 1980, the year of my ordination, and 1985. I was sorely disappointed, however, when that emphasis did not happen. My European American sisters proceeded with their celebration but failed to note that we ordained women of color, along with our unique gifts, were not a part of the event.

I patiently waited for the affirmation of both our ministry and gifts that I was certain would come with the twentieth anniversary celebration. By 1990 Native American and Asian sisters had been ordained. I was again disappointed.

As plans are now underway for the 25th anniversary celebration I no longer look to my European American sisters for either acknowledgement of or affirmation toward women of color. In this manner I will not be disappointed.

Most of my ordained European American sisters seem unaware of the both the issues and experiences of their ordained sisters of color unless those issues and experiences are directly related to the European American community. If we raise issues that are critical to the survival of our respective communities and our ministries, we become the problem and the resources by which we might address those issues dry up. The issues with which the European American community wrestles ultimately become the *a priori* issues for every community: sexual harassment, sexuality and sexual orientation, inclusive language, political power and ambition, feminist theology, and jockeying for ecclesiastical position, to name a few.

For the record, these issues do affect our communities but not in the endemic way in which the European American community is affected by them. All of our communities have people of both genders who are homophobic, use sexist language, and are politically ambitious. But the primary issues with which communities of color wrestle are those connected with our very survival: poverty, violence, religious and political self-determinism, indigenous leadership training, and racism.

Racism affects our relationships when many of our European American sisters and brothers perceive God's gifts of racial and ethnic diversity as inferior, valueless, and worthless. The European roots of our church are often the standard by which we judge that which is Lutheran and that which is not. My European American sisters are safe ideologically and will maintain Lutheran historical orthodoxy. If people of color do not conform to, affirm, and celebrate Lutheranism's northern European roots at the expense of our unique cultural expressions, we are perceived as either non- or anti-Lutheran. People of color have repeatedly stated that dispassionate Scandinavian worship styles and German confessional theology cannot be the only standards by which our communities and ministries are judged.

Another example of how racism affects relationships, particularly among women, is when one woman of color is chosen as more acceptable than another. She is selected by the European American community as the leader or the model for the rest of us and we are charged to become more like her. The irony is that if the one chosen had not performed in a manner consistent with the values and standards set by the community doing the selecting she would have never been chosen in the first place.

CHERYL STEWART PERO

Canadian author Margaret Atwood, in *The Handmaid's Tale*, characterizes this as an act of oppression. A person from the oppressed group is selected to act as the overseer of the oppressed; self-interest insures that the one to oversee will be more oppressive to her sisters that the oppressor herself.

The examples of racism cited here have tragic consequences. Because my European American sisters benefit from white privilege, they successfully divert the liberation movements from men and women of color to themselves. Our church's institutions and agencies collude in that diversion by evading affirmative action guidelines developed to assist people of color with ministry opportunities. Instead of opening doors to people of color, staff call and hire greater numbers of European American women. People of color are neither pursued nor encouraged to fill positions with the same intensity as are European American women. My European American sisters are consistently being placed in positions where they are charged with the task to build an inclusive church and given the portfolios by which to make it happen. The relationships among all women however, are compromised by their efforts. Our diversity becomes deprived of value both as a community and as individuals.

Racism also has negative consequences on our language as a community of women. For at least fifteen years I have asked that European American women be clear about whom they speak when they generically refer to "women." The women to whom they refer usually do not include or reflect the thoughts of women of color. As my foremother, Sojourner Truth, asked: "Ain't I a woman?" Inclusive language for women of color is more than simply substituting for masculine pronouns. For language to be inclusive there must be a reformation of language and thought patterns that give ethnic/racial offense or presume that European American women can speak for all women. To be sure, there are significant differences among feminist and womanist theologies, Asian women's theology, Native American spirituality, and mujerista theology.

Women of color are about the business of changing this *modus operandi*. We are building multicultural communities because we are multicultural women.

When women of color gather, such as we did recently in San Antonio, Texas, at the second historic meeting of ordained women of color of the Evangelical Lutheran Church in America (ELCA), it is reassuring to hear the similar pain in our stories and to celebrate our joys in the midst of pain. At that event a network for women of color was forged and a call was issued for reconciliation, reciprocity, respect, and accountability among all ordained women in the ELCA.

In marking the twenty-fifth anniversary celebration of Lutheran women in ordained ministry, it is my hope the ministries of women of color might be celebrated by every Lutheran as ministries of the ELCA. If we cannot be equal partners in celebrating these significant milestones as multicultural milestones of the ELCA, we are not sisters and brothers in the Christian faith.

In the meantime I remain a pragmatist, I suppose. I see this celebration through a particular set of historical lenses that make it somewhat analogous to another historical event. In response to the 1852 Fourth of July celebration in Rochester, New York, my forefather the eloquent orator Frederick Douglass gave a speech on July 5 entitled "American Slavery." I close with a quote from his text. The parenthetical words are mine, words in italic are his.

> What have I, or those I represent, to do with your national (celebration)? . . . I am not included within the pale of this glorious anniversary! Your high (celebration) only reveals the immeasurable distance between us. The blessings in which you, this day rejoice, are not enjoyed in common. The rich inheritance . . . bequeathed by your fathers is shared by you, not by me. . . . This (celebration) is *yours, not mine. You* may rejoice, I must mourn . . . (sisters), above your national tumultous joy, I hear the mournful wail of millions whose chains . . . are rendered more intolerable by the jubilee shouts that reach them.[2]

I trust that the 30th anniversary will be different for those who are coming after me.

Notes

1. Margaret Herz-Lane, "The Magnificent Seven," *Lutheran Women in Ordained Ministry 1970-1995: Reflections and Perspectives* (Minneapolis: Augsburg Books, 1995), pp. 79-85. Text identifies early women of color who were among the first to be ordained in the LCA.

2. *Early American Negro Writers: Selections with Biographical and Critical Introductions*, ed. Benjamin Brawley, (New York: Dover Publications, Inc., 1970), pp. 202-204.

THE OPENING DOOR OF PENTECOST
April Ulring Larson

THE WORD HAD GOTTEN OUT! The women of the church were abuzz. After a series of seven excellent male interns, this congregation was now assigned its first female. People were on all sides of this issue, but everyone agreed on one matter: Nellie would be upset. Nellie was the conservative grand matriarch of the congregation. Now in her eighties, she was still able to outwork any young whippersnapper in the church kitchen. So the women, knowing what her answer would be, turned to Nellie and asked her what she thought. Nellie spoke, " 'In the last days it will be, God declares, that I will pour out my Spirit upon all flesh, and your sons and your daughters shall prophesy (Acts 2:17).' " There was silence in the kitchen!

The voices of women have been silenced in the public church over the ages. On the pages of this volume, a few of these voices speak, sharing an event of history, a history dramatically changed. On these pages a gender once silenced now speaks giving honor to centuries of women who have spoken and acted at great personal cost; women who without public voice have remained faithful to the Gospel.

These pages mark an attempt to hear half of the church speak—speak not just for that half, but for the whole church. In ages past our forefathers wrote and exclusively defined all sacred and confessional documents. Councils of our forefathers decided the boundaries between truth and heresy apart from women's experiences of faith. Still today, on the basis of the history of the faith defined by only our fathers, the faith of our mothers, our sisters, our daughters, and our sons is judged. Over the ages, in the church's public arena and in the scriptures, the voices of women's witness, reflection, and theology seldom spoke. If these voices spoke, they were often not believed or heard (Luke 24:11). Even less often were they recorded and when recorded they were frequently misinterpreted.

Yes, the church is abuzz as women bring forth their gifts, women's gifts. Hands, eyes, ears previously not welcomed are now welcome and empowered in the public worship and discourse in many parts of the church of Jesus Christ.

"Women of the late twentieth century are revolutionizing the most sexist institution in history—organized religion," according to Patricia Aburdene and John Naisbitt in *Megatrends for Women* (Villard Books/Random House,1992). However, for Christians this revolution began with Jesus and the way Jesus treated women in the patriarchal society of the first century.

Jesus made it clear there was to be no discrimination in who was given the authority to preach, teach, and evangelize. Mary Magdalene was sent forth by Jesus as the first witness to the resurrection and as an apostle to the apostles with the words, "Go to my brothers and say to them "(John 20:17-18; see also Matthew and Mark). The Samaritan woman with whom Jesus had his longest theological discussion recorded in Scripture became the first evangelist (see John 4). And it is Martha who makes an apostolic confession prior to the raising of Lazarus from the dead: "I believe that you are the Messiah, the Son of God, the one coming into the world (John 11:27; compare with Peter's confession in Matthew, Mark, and Luke.)

Nevertheless, it was almost two thousand years after Jesus that the wall in Christian churches keeping women from entering the "holy of holies" was removed. In the Evangelical Lutheran Church in America (ELCA) that barrier was eliminated not with the election of its first woman bishop, but at the ordination of the first woman pastor. Given the understanding in the Lutheran church that there is one office of ordained ministry (pastor/ bishop) the dividing wall was taken down when our predecessor bodies decided in 1970 to ordain women. Few knew then how dramatically that event would change the church. I am proud of and thankful to my church for taking that decisive step, acknowledging in a new way that both sexes are equally made in the image of God (Genesis 1:27) and that both sexes are equally able to represent the holy.

The decision to ordain women was made twenty-five years ago. Over the years, we have been in dialogue with other denominations that hold the three-fold office of ministry (bishops, pastors, and deacons) but do not accept women as pastors or bishops. Prior to the Lutheran election of women bishops, it was conceivable these denominations might agree to join with the ELCA as long as we kept the office of bishop exclusively male. Thus the rubble of that dividing wall against women could have remained, apart from the election of women bishops.

An Orthodox patriarch called the election of the first Lutheran women bishop in the U.S. "dividing" because Orthodox members of the U.S. Lutheran and Orthodox dialogues were not consulted first. However, once the Lutheran church ordained women as pastors, it was only a matter of time until women bishops would be elected as part of the one office of pastor/ bishop. Yes, this reaction of one of our dialogue partners does indicate the importance of the election of women as bishops. Any who harbored doubts of the liberating effect of the election of women bishops had only to come to my living room after my election on June 12, 1992. It was filled with flowers, and I wasn't even dead!

The power of this event is in the symbol. The first element is: There is no place in church structure or in the "holy of holies" that women cannot enter. Women, even women who are not virgins and who are "unclean," can bear the holy (that is, preach the Word and preside at the Eucharist and Baptism). With the election of the first Lutheran woman bishop in the world, Bishop Maria Jepsen, we say to all the faith communions, "We now have and are committed in the future to having women in all offices of the ordained ministry."[1]

The second element of this symbol is: The female is granted permission by the church (the holy community) to stand for all humanity. Our children learn the opposite early in life, where even most of the Sesame Street characters are male. Translated into the church, this societal practice of using only men to represent corporate humanity has meant that only the male can stand on behalf of the community and offer prayers to the triune God. Thus the power of the symbol of woman as pastor and bishop: She can publicly speak the word of God and administer the body and blood of Christ for all the people of God. She can stand in the chancel, the "holy of holies," and bring the prayers of both men and women. Her prayer, her interpretation of their pain and experiences, stands not only for women, but for the whole community, male and female.

One continues to see barriers to the full expression of the gifts of over half of the members of the church. The ordination of women and the election of women bishops might have been only a temporary matter if it weren't for the biblical scholars and women theologians who walk side by side with them, interpreting Scripture in light of the whole human experience (now including, for the first time, the experiences of women). This is a difficult task, especially since women have little recorded history and have grown up learning to defer to the male experience as though it were the only human experience.

I am thankful that more of my male colleagues (pastors and bishops) are realizing that the majority of members in their parishes experience life and God through a different set of lenses than the dominant culture; these colleagues are including women theologians and theologians from other contexts in their reading. They are beginning to become sensitive to and to share vicariously in the experience of the majority of the people who sit in our pews: women who experience life differently than they are "expected" to experience it.

Having women bishops opens the door just a bit wider, so the full range of the gifts and experiences of people with God and the world is now included in the oversight of the church. May the door continue to swing wider so that our church is seen for what it already is: no longer a monolithic structure, but a multicultural communion—the essence of Pentecost. "In the last days it will be, God declares, that I will pour out my Spirit upon all flesh, and your sons and daughters shall prophesy" (Acts 2:17).

Notes

1. Maria Jepsen was elected bishop of The North Elbian Church in Hamburg, Germany in April, 1992. Since the elections of Jepsen and Larson, three other women have been elected as bishops, one in Norway, one in Denmark, and one in South Dakota.

Portions of this article were first printed in an article called "Face to Face" in *Word and World* 13 (Summer 1993), pp. 302-307. The authors of that article were Maria Jebson and April Larson.

PERSISTENT VOICES CHAMPION
THE INCLUSION OF WOMEN
Mary Ann Moller-Gunderson

WHEN I WAS A SENIOR SEMINARIAN in 1977, the seminary I attended had a process that seniors jokingly referred to as the "the meat market." Bishops from across the Lutheran Church in America (LCA) were invited to come and meet those of us who were graduating. We all met at a reception in a large room. Plan A, if we were candidates, was to meet and impress the bishops from the synods that were among our top three choices for a call. Most of us felt a bit like cattle being paraded before meat buyers. If we were successful, we left the reception with an appointment for a private conversation with the bishop of choice about a possible call. If not, we needed to scramble to formulate plan B and arrange to talk with a bishop of another synod.

I personally had to work both plan A and plan B. The first bishop I spoke to said, "I do not now, nor will I ever, have room in my synod for an ordained woman or for a clergy couple." If nothing else, that bishop was quite clear about his personal policy regarding the placement of women. Next, I visited with the bishop from my home synod. Bishop A.G. Fjellman said, "Because you are a daughter of the Northwest, it is my duty to do everything in my power to see that you receive a call to a parish in our synod. Just telephone me a month before you graduate, and I will take it from there." Bishop Fjellman kept his word. I phoned him a month before graduation; within three weeks, I had a call to serve as pastor of a congregation in the Pacific Northwest Synod.

These two encounters with bishops bracket the effect of the ordination of women on the polity and policy of the Evangelical Lutheran Church in America (ELCA) and its predecessor church bodies. Like the parable of the persistent widow and the unjust judge (Luke 18:1-8), it has required steadfastness on the part of the whole church to make the ordination of women move from an acceptable action on the convention floor in 1970 to actual policy. Fortunately, along the way God has raised up persistent voices that have championed the inclusion of women in ministry in every expression of the church.

For those of us ordained in the first decade after the predecessor church bodies made their decision to permit the ordination of women, the early years were a kind of "salting with fire" (Mark 9:49). The LCA had voted a new polity for itself in 1970. Our governing documents were changed by convention action to affirm that God could, by the power of the Holy Spirit, call women to the ministry of Word and Sacrament. This was a monumental decision that would forever alter the shape of ministry within much of Lutheranism. During the 1970s, many in the church perhaps did not anticipate that our policies would also need reshaping in order for the church to fully enact its decision to ordain women.

I have come to believe that policy changes are actually far more elusive than monumental constitutional changes, in that policy includes both the *intent* and the *will* to act. Few of us would argue, for example, against a twenty-mile-per-hour speed limit within a school zone. We readily accept the law set before us by those who govern. But actually slowing the car down to drive only twenty miles per hour requires unfailing resolve and vigilance on the part of the driver.

This is the realm of *policy*: to intentionally abide by procedures that propel us into a chosen course of action. Bishop Fjellman had an unwritten policy that placement of daughters and sons from the Pacific Northwest was the responsibility of the bishop of that synod. He consistently lived out that policy, whether the candidate was male or female. It was the resolve of the bishop that fueled his unwritten, but, nevertheless, firm policy to place women pastors from the Pacific Northwest in his synod.

Policy is also dictated by *attitude* and the *will* to proceed with what we have declared that we will do. Attitudes escape legislation; one cannot force the heart. This means that attitudes are the birthplace of most *unwritten* policies. Notice the emphasis on the word <u>unwritten</u>. Very few among us are blatantly biased anymore about excluding women as leaders in the church. Our written policies have been revised, yet attitudes of exclusion remain. Attitudes are, therefore, tough to reform. I have often wondered if we as a church were prepared for the attitudinal resistance throughout the church in response to the decision to ordain women. That resistance sabotaged, and in some places continues to block, the leadership of women in the church.

The bishop whose spoken policy was that he would never have room for an ordained woman or clergy couple in his synod had no intention of enacting the decision of the LCA convention to ordain women. His attitudes dictated the policies of his synod. There were no requirements that a bishop had to submit the names of women to a congregation engaged in a call process. Nor were congregations expected to interview all candidates whose names had been submitted. This meant that bias quickly reared its head.

Especially in the first decade of the ordination of women, it was policy matters like those governing the call process that proved again to be the salting with fire for many women clergy. History is replete with examples of women whose names were not submitted for consideration by call committees. One female candidate was told that she was too attractive to receive a call. The bishop of that synod never did submit her name to a congregation. Bishops regularly told women candidates that the congregations in their synod were just not ready for a female pastor. In that first decade, long waits for a call were normative for women.

There were labor pains at the congregational level as well. The most frequent bias seemed to occur in the process of screening candidates. Call committees often refused to interview a woman. Sometimes the committee went through the motions of the interview, but did not recommend the woman to the congregation.

In some tragic cases, women who were recommended to a congregation by the call committee did not receive the necessary two-thirds majority vote by the congregation. The reason given almost always had to do with gender. The absence of effective policies regarding the call process caused enormous frustration and pain for many women clergy.

In my second call, I am told, someone asked during the congregational meeting if the Bible barred women from serving as pastors. A highly respected man answered: "The Bible says a woman can be a pastor as long as it is okay with her husband." So I was issued the call to that congregation. Not all of my colleagues were so fortunate. Biblical and theological questions were difficult for many congregations to negotiate. In the early years, the church lacked effective resources to teach members about these theologically driven gender issues. In addition, most people had never met a female pastor. What would she sound like? What would she wear? I recall an experience when I wore my clerical collar to the grocery store. A complete stranger approached me and asked, "What are you?" The lack of female clergy as role models, the absence of biblical and theological teaching tools, and the newness of women clergy all required a period of living into our decision to ordain women.

While it was a monumental decision for the predecessor church bodies to change their *polity* or church governance to include approval of the ordination of women, the church has been plodding at a revision of *policy* ever since. Webster's Dictionary defines plodding as "working laboriously." As one who has worked for the congregational, synodical, and churchwide expressions of the church, I can attest that our labor has required steadfast attention to matters of policy. No expression of the church has been exempt.

When I was a student at the seminary, for example, I vividly recall one of the professors who stated that he was not in favor of the ordination of women and believed that the church had erred in adopting the 1970 resolution. It was difficult to hear

MARY ANN MOLLER-GUNDERSON

the professor publicly state his opposition seven years after the church had made its decision, and with women in the classroom. We knew he had a right to his own theological position. However, we could not help but hear that the women present were, in his opinion, a "mistake" for the church. Such comments were not uncommon at the time. Most seminaries had not yet grappled with the deeper realities which root our policies in exclusive behaviors. The attitudes and the will of some of the faculty as well as their biblical and theological positions had an impact on the experience of women students.

Unwritten policies also govern congregational life. My first call was to serve as co-pastor, with my husband, of a congregation in a synod that had only one other female pastor. We were told that at the congregational meeting the vote was one short of the required two-thirds majority to issue the call. The congregation's president then voted to achieve the majority—and we received the call to serve as their pastors.

It required tenacity on the part of that call committee and president to put flesh on the polity of the LCA to ordain women. In the early years of women's ordination, there were numerous instances when congregations were put to the test to enact policies which were commensurate with our denominational polity. Thank God for the risk-takers among us. They created a toehold for women as we sought to reshape the policies imbedded in church practice.

Like moments in the parish, there were kairos moments during my tenure as an assistant to the bishop in the Greater Milwaukee Synod. Bishop Peter Rogness had a clearly-stated policy to advocate for placement of women clergy in the synod. We thought we had the necessary procedures in place to accomplish that goal. When we brought the names of three candidates to call committees, we often submitted the names of women. But much to our disappointment, even if only one candidate was male, call committees chose the man in all but one case. We learned once again that the policy required intentionality on our part to establish and abide by procedures which could propel us toward the placement of women. As a staff, we had underestimated the acidity of the soil in some congregations regarding women clergy. We were up against deeply ingrained attitudes: "So long as she doesn't serve here in our congregation, women clergy are fine."

When we changed our procedures with call committees, our synodical policy finally upheld our decision as a denomination. We still submitted three names to call committees. The difference was our requirement that call committees had to interview all three candidates. Much to our satisfaction, we discovered that call committees who interviewed both women and men selected a woman half of the time.

We also set out to enhance the receptivity to women in call processes beyond the call committee. If our policy was to yield the fruit of women serving as pastors in congregations, we needed procedures for influencing congregational attitudes as well. A series of cottage meetings, morning coffees, or "meet the candidate" events within the congregation led to far greater placement of women in the synod. Once again, we learned that enacting policy required plodding, working laboriously as a synod staff. It was something like the persistent widow approaching the unjust judge one more time. Finally the risk-takers and affirmative voices within congregations prevailed and women received the call.

Having recently been a member of the churchwide staff, I saw yet too many places in the church where women are not represented at the table. Hopefully, we are on the threshold of seeing numbers of women called to serve as seminary presidents, as presidents of our Lutheran colleges and universities, as executives of churchwide organization units, as senior pastors of large congregations, as bishops, and as pastor developers of new congregations.

My dream is that one day soon we will be part of a church where key leadership positions are shared equally by women and men. The church will need to persevere in policy and behavior to make this happen. It will take courageous advocacy on the part of women and men to make equal partnership in the ministry of Jesus Christ a reality. We are not yet there, but the tenacity of the persistent widow remains a powerful mentor for a church committed to full sharing of the leadership gifts of all God's children.

LUTHERAN WOMEN IN THEOLOGICAL STUDIES: HEADWAY, HARD WORK, HURT, AND HOPE

Phyllis Anderson

IN SEPARATE REPORTS of studies on women's ordination in 1970 and 1972, Raymond Tiemeyer (on staff in the Lutheran Church in America [LCA]) and Joseph Burgess (former executive director for the Division of Theological Studies, Lutheran Council in the USA [LCUSA]) each expressed confidence that a decision to ordain women would have little practical impact. Very few women, they predicted, would actually seek ordination and prepare to be pastors.[1]

They could not have been more wrong. As soon as the Lutheran churches in North America made the decision to ordain women in 1970, women started coming to seminary. At first it was just a trickle—there were one or two in a class. Women's voices were lost in the deep, male sound of worship in the seminary chapel. With exceptions too rare to mention, the curriculum was determined and taught by men.

Today more than forty percent of the students and twenty percent of the faculty at seminaries in the Evangelical Lutheran Church in America (ELCA) are women.[2] Women are challenging traditional interpretations of Scripture, conceptions of authority, and the nature of theological discourse itself. Historians of religion will count women's influence on church leadership and theological scholarship among the most significant and far-reaching developments in the western church in this century.

These have been twenty-five years of rapid transition. The influx of women in theological education testifies to God's persistence in calling women to ministry, to the faithfulness and courage of the women who overcame personal and structural barriers to answer that call, and to the elasticity of institutions that have been stretched in the process of preparing these women for ministry. Transitional years, however, are hard.

At twenty-five years we celebrate the headway that has been made not only for the women pastors, theologians and theology students, but also for God's mission being carried forward through them. While the focus of this volume is on the gains for women, the gain and the glory are finally God's. When the gifts of women are utilized in theological scholarship and pastoral ministry, they help to build up the whole body of Christ. When their contributions are thwarted, the body suffers, because some perspectives on God's word and God's activity in our world are lost. While this book is a reflection on the ordination of Lutheran women, it is a story of the whole church as it seeks to embody in every aspect of its life an inclusive vision of the people of God. On the way to that vision there have been headway, hard work, hurt, and hope.

HEADWAY

Students. Theological education in North America has changed more in the past twenty-five years than in the previous two hundred.[3] Overall, seminarians are more often female, second-career, part-time. They come from more diverse backgrounds and are dispersed among a variety of academic programs leading to different vocational goals. In 1992, only sixty percent of students at ELCA seminaries and forty-five percent of students at all North American seminaries were pursuing Master of Divinity (M.Div.) degrees, the program that normally leads to ordination.[4] The advent of women on campus has been a major factor in each of the major demographic changes in seminaries.

More female. Women contributed significantly to the increase in enrollment at Protestant seminaries during the 1970s and

1980s. The enrollment of women in M.Div. programs has increased more rapidly than the overall enrollment in such programs. To put it another way, fewer men are preparing for pastoral ministry than prior to 1970. Were it not for the women, the ELCA and other Protestant denominations would be experiencing a shortage of pastors.

More second-career. Seminary student bodies today are generally more mature and experienced. This is particularly true for women. At the eight ELCA seminaries in 1992, fifty-eight percent of female M.Div. candidates were over thirty-five years old, in contrast with thirty-seven percent of the male M.Div. candidates.[5]

More part-time. Fewer students are able to pursue theological education as a full-time, residential experience. While the total number of students at ELCA seminaries rose modestly during the 1980s, the combined full-time equivalent (FTE) enrollment of the eight seminaries actually dropped from 2264 to 1861 during that period.[6] Because of family responsibilities or financial pressures, more women than men attend seminary part-time.

One can cite church leaders in every age bemoaning the poor quality of ministerial candidates. If intelligence is a criteria for ministerial competency, there is new reason for complaint. The average intelligence of entering seminarians as measured by the Graduate Record Examination (GRE) has decreased over the last twenty-five years. In contrast to this general trend, the average scores for entering women seminarians are not only higher than those of their male counterparts, but also higher than the average for women entering other professions.[7]

Faculty. Institutions have responded gradually and sometimes reluctantly to these changes in the student population. It soon became evident that seminaries, in response to this change, would have to provide women faculty who could begin to modify the ethos and serve as role models for women students.

Several seminaries could boast a woman librarian or faculty member somewhere in their past. Between 1910 and 1914, Jennie Bloom Summers taught Latin, German, English, and psychology at Pacific Theological Seminary, then located in Portland,

Oregon. Bertha Paulson was professor of sociology of religion at Lutheran Theological Seminary at Gettysburg from 1945 to 1963. In 1970, however, there were no women serving in tenure-eligible positions on the faculties of the seminaries that eventually became part of the ELCA. In 1971, Jean Bozeman began teaching Christian education at the Lutheran School of Theology at Chicago, and in 1975 was also appointed dean of students. Margaret Krych, another in the field of Christian education, was appointed to a tenure-eligible teaching post at The Lutheran School of Theology at Philadelphia in 1977. She was the first ordained woman to be granted faculty status at a Lutheran seminary. In 1978, Faith Burgess (now Rohrbough) joined Krych on the faculty in Philadelphia as academic dean and associate professor in American church history. And in 1979, Norma Cook Everist joined faculty at Wartburg Theological Seminary, Dubuque, Iowa, as a teacher of educational ministry and church administration. This was the first appointment of a woman to a tenure-eligible position in the American Lutheran Church.

Today approximately twenty percent of the combined ELCA seminary faculties, are women. Furthermore, according to the 1993-94 Directory of Lutheran Doctoral Candidates in Theological Disciplines, forty-five women and forty-five men are presently earning the necessary academic credentials for teaching positions in seminaries or college religion departments.[8]

While no women currently serve as academic deans or presidents of ELCA seminaries, women increasingly hold cabinet-level positions in student services and finance. The denominational executive for theological education in the ELCA is an ordained woman. At least one-third of the boards of the ELCA seminaries are women, and one of them currently serves as board chair.

Teaching and Learning. Changes are slowly taking place in the seminary curriculum and within the classroom. In Lutheran seminaries, the academic track for ordination candidates consists primarily of required courses. Many of these basic courses now intentionally include sections on issues related to women and texts written by women. Students taking general curricular offerings may pursue particular interests in women's history or theological perspectives in research papers or collateral reading. If courses dealing specifically with women in ministry or feminist theology are offered, they are usually electives. Seminaries intentionally seek out women pastors to serve as supervisors for students in field placements, internship, and clinical pastoral education, but these numbers remain small.

These changes, while not radical, represent significant headway since my senior year in seminary in 1976. At that time a male faculty member served by default as acting "dean of women." The four women in the senior class had to design and teach their own January interim course if they were going to have any acquaintance with women's perspectives in theology before completing seminary studies.

HARD WORK AND HURT

Despite the headway that has been made, seminary continues to be an alienating environment for many women students and faculty members. The changes instituted to accommodate women students and faculty have largely been directed toward creating a place for women in a world traditionally shaped by male patterns. From the point of view of women students, Lutheran seminaries still seem to be largely oriented toward single, male, residential students. The scheduling of classes and field work and the expectations for extra-curricular involvement do not fully take into account the family and work responsibilities of older, part-time students. Adult learning models are only gradually being introduced, often by women faculty. Classes overall remain more content centered than learner centered. Single women with children, as a group, leave seminary with the highest level of financial indebtedness.[9]

It has never been easy to organize women seminarians as a distinctive and cohesive group. Women entering seminary are typically focused more on their vocational goals and academic challenges than on their identity as women. They are glad for the opportunity to study and not eager to set themselves apart from their male colleagues. Those who come with a strong feminist orientation from their college studies or life experience are often disappointed at the lack of feminist activism on campus.

In the course of studying Scripture, church history, theology, preaching, pastoral care, and other fields, more and more women are forced to come to terms with the extent to which their experience has been excluded from the church's story. For some women the required parish internship becomes the occasion when they discover both the subtle discrimination and the unique ministry opportunities that come to them as women.

Women students in 1995, no less than in 1970, need opportunities to reflect with others on what difference being a woman makes to the study of theology and to ministry. The bonds they form with one another in seminary sustain many women pastors over long-distance telephone lines through the challenging, often lonely years in ministry.

Women who aspire to seminary teaching also have their share of hard work and hurt. While seminaries are actively seeking women candidates for faculty positions, many women still feel disadvantaged in job searches. Because their lives have not followed the standard developmental model of their male counterparts, they may not have the traditional credentials for teaching at a Lutheran seminary: denominational identity, ordination, parish experience, and broad competence in the basic academic disciplines that are central to the seminary curriculum. Just as women begin to accumulate the appropriate credentials, many schools must reduce rather than add faculty positions due to financial pressures.

Even if a woman does get the job, she often continues to feel disadvantaged. Her own insecurities are exacerbated in a male-dominated environment where she needs to establish herself through authoritative teaching, sometimes combative intellectual arguments with faculty colleagues, and focused research that results in publication. In some cases, because of the institution's need to add women to the faculty, women have received faculty appointments before completing dissertations or before they have had a chance to serve in parish ministry. Lutheran seminaries have hired more women than men who are not ordained or who

PHYLLIS ANDERSON

are members of other denominations. What begins as affirmative action may work against women when tenure is considered.

Too many women are in part-time or quasi-administrative roles that are not eligible for tenure. Some women must take such positions to accommodate family needs or because that is all that is offered. Others choose such situations in order to break the traditional mold or because they are unwilling to make the kind of personal sacrifice and political calculation required for building a traditional academic career.

Consequently the small but growing minority of women on most seminary campuses sense that they are less likely than their male colleagues to gain tenure, become fully integrated into the power structure of the faculty, or be elected to major administrative posts. Indeed this pattern has been confirmed across higher education in North America.[10]

HOPE: IT WILL TAKE TIME

It will take still more time before we have a critical mass of senior women faculty and administrators in our ELCA seminaries. But that is where the hope lies for the transformation of Lutheran theological education to make it a more trustworthy and empowering place for women.

Women who have passed all the hurdles to full tenured faculty status and have a few strong women colleagues experience the seminary environment quite differently than they did as students or junior faculty. Many testify to a profound change in their own confidence in the classroom, their freedom to research and write on controversial topics related to women's concerns, and their power to publicly interpret the Christian story through the lenses women's experience brings. They have found a voice in the institution and they have a long-term stake in the future of the institution. We depend on such women to be committed and courageous in using that hard-won voice to raise again and again the difficult and wearisome questions about the place of all women in these institutions, in the church, and in the world.

Further progress will require continued hard work from women and from the institutions in which they study and teach. It is going to hurt. It will take an extra measure of hope to keep working and praying for a reality that most of us will not experience in our own lifetime.

Notes

1. Raymond Tiemeyer, The Ordination of Women (Minneapolis: Augsburg Books, 1973), pp. 44-45. Joseph A. Burgess, *Can Women Serve in the Ordained Ministry?* (Minneapolis: Augsburg Books, 1973), p. 15.

2. ELCA enrollment statistics compiled annually by the ELCA Division for Ministry.

3. Joseph P. O'Neill and Richard T. Murphy, "Changing Age and Gender Profiles among Entering Seminary Students: 1975-1989." *Ministry Research Notes*, Spring 1991, Princeton: Educational Testing Service, p. 2.

4. ELCA enrollment statistics compiled annually by the ELCA Division for Ministry and the *Fact Book on Theological Education*, published annually by the Association of Theological Schools in the United States and Canada, Pittsburgh, Pennsylvania.

5. *Ibid.*

6. Joseph P. O'Neill, "Denominational Funding of Theological Education," unpublished article, July, 1995.

7. O'Neill and Murphy, *op. cit.*

8. 1993-1994 Directory of Lutheran Doctoral Candidates in Theological Disciplines (available from ELCA Division for Ministry).

9. Anthony Ruger and Barbara Wheeler, "Deeper in Debt: Are Seminary Students Borrowing Too Much?", *The Christian Century*, February 2-9, 1994, p. 101.

10. Paula Caplan, *Lifting a Ton of Feathers: A Woman's Guide to Surviving in the Academic World.* (Toronto: University of Toronto Press, 1993), pp. 177-180.

THERE WAS MORE TO IT THAN I THOUGHT AND THERE IS EVEN MORE TO COME: RETROSPECTIVE PROSPECTS

Krister Stendahl

I GET NERVOUS when theologians—both women and men—claim that the ordination of women is not a question of justice or of equality or of emancipation. Such disclaimers grow out of feelings that the church should be about love, and that mere justice somehow is sub-Christian; or that the very idea of rights comes from the Enlightenment and not from the Gospel. It could be argued and exemplified that, by and large, theologians find it difficult to be one hundred percent excited about justice. The reason is, I guess, that justice is too universal, it has no Christian specificity. We never say "Christian justice," but we certainly say "Christian love." It takes a generous heart and mind to be devoted to what is not one's special thing.

Why this way to begin my reflections? For I have been asked to think about what might happen in the church when the pool for ordained ministry suddenly has doubled, and that in the very generation when we happen to be around? No doubt this is one of the greatest events in church history, well in class with the Reformation.

My reason for starting as I do is this. One of the dynamics that led up to the change, and will continue as a dialectic in the years to come, is the interplay between equality and justice on the one hand, and the differences and complimentarity of female and male realities on the other. It seems clear to me that equality and justice must come first as the spearhead that opens up insulated structures. At that point, if one stresses the complementarity too much, one cannot avoid the "separate but equal" syndrome so infamous in the history of the emancipation of African Americans. That is why it was and is important to see the ordination of women as part of women's emancipation. One would have liked it to have been a first and pioneering part of that liberation, but let us at least—and at last—hail it as the sign of its consolidation.[1]

Once there is a reasonable level of acceptance in the church of the rights of women to be equal with men, those very rights transform themselves into the right to be different, and a new era has dawned in both theology and church life for both women and men. When we had an all-male clergy, somehow we men pretended to be universally human when we were mere males. The English language gave it to us: Man meant humankind—but it does not really anymore.

To speak about gender differences—in ways of thinking; in spirituality; in understandings of God, of faith, of love, of eros and agape—is difficult indeed. One tends to fall back on the very stereotypes that were engendered by a male-dominated culture. Hence I should stop right here and tell myself and the brethren to shut up until the sisters have had enough time and space to deconstruct and reconstruct ways to recognize and celebrate diversities as gifts to one another, to the communities of faith, and to the society at large. But I was asked to write.

I think we underestimate how radical and deep a shift in the conscious and unconscious theological paradigms we face when women become equal players in the arts of preaching, teaching, liturgy, and administration. In any case, that was true for me when I wrote my first pieces on the role of women and the issues of women's ordination. That was in the early 1950s, back in Sweden. I was drawn into the debate when a government-appointed study commission reported favorably on the ordination of women. As a chaplain to students and a New Testament doctoral student in a *sola scriptura* church and culture I felt the challenge. To me that challenge was one of hermeneutics. For it was clear to me that the emancipation of women was right, and to think of the church and its priesthood as "the exception" to that rule was unbearable. But it was equally clear to me that there were stark statements in the Bible, and especially in the New Testament, that forbade women the roles of teaching or of leadership in the church. The most explicit one was of course in 1 Timothy 2:9-15, the Magna Carta for the "*Kinder-Küche-Kirche*" womanhood, once actually functioning as a liberation of women from inferiority over against the religious life of nuns; remember Käthe Luther.

Unfortunately, I was not impressed by the "liberal" method of stressing that such words about women as more susceptible to the assault of Satan, and so forth, were not Paul's own, since they are found in the certainly pseudo-Pauline Pastoral Epistles. I would agree that 1 Corinthians 14:34-36 probably is a later church addition to the text, but it is still in the Bible. Nor was I convinced by the various attempts at distinguishing between what is culturally conditioned and what are "timeless truths" in the Bible, for I think every word of Scripture is conditioned by the time and space of its origin. Even if "ordination" in our sense has no exact equivalent in Paul's churches, I thought he would have been against it for women. That is why for me the question was one of hermeneutics.

There is the analogy in the overcoming of slavery in spite of slaves being basically accepted by Paul as part of the world. For me it became important to recognize Paul's vision of how even the human dichotomy of male and female is transcended in Christ. Galatians 3:28, the crucial verse, is actually more striking than most translations allow for. A literal translation would read:

> There is neither Jew nor Greek, there is neither slave nor free, there is not "male and female," for you are all one in Christ Jesus.

The change in syntax from "neither/nor" to "not" makes it clear that Paul quotes Genesis 1:27, transcending the very structure of human reality. This transcending vision of Paul's should be lifted up and not squelched, dulled, annulled, or homogenized by reference to the passages where Paul did not quite see the consequences of his vision. Perhaps he was a better theologian than social ethicist. That would not be unique in the history of theology.

Nor was I impressed by the argument, now almost canonized by Pope John Paul II, that the incarnation in the male Jesus Christ requires that the priests representing Christ must likewise be males. To which one could then ask if priests have to be Jews. The jewishness of Jesus might actually be theologically more significant than his gender.

For me all this did add up to my conviction that the question was one of hermeneutics.[2] To put it sharply: I guess Paul was/would be against it, but that does not quite settle the matter. His very insight of equal status in Christ, his theological vision that goes against the grain of his own habits of thought, became for me a way toward a hermeneutic ever suspicious of homogenization. Actually, it was on the anvil of the 1950s debate in Sweden that I hammered out the method of interpretation that has guided my writing and teaching through the decades. When we withstand the apologetic temptation to have the various texts say the same thing, then the Bible comes alive and what Paul says, in spite of himself, becomes most precious.

In the Church of Sweden the debates and decisions led to the first ordination of women on Palm Sunday 1960. In Sweden that was well before the impact of the women's liberation movement. There was not yet a women's theology. The hermeneutics of suspicion had not raised our consciousness as to gender and systemic sexism. For the first women ordained—in the U.S. as in Sweden—the only role models were those of male clergy. To be sure, there was an awareness that women had special gifts. To men, and hence for the decisionmakers in the church, this suggested that women were best at the ministries of caring, which now meant pastoral care rather than preaching, liturgy, and leadership. Such stereotyping still accounts for the shockingly small number of women as senior pastors in large, multi-staff congregations.

I do not expect all women clergy to be flaming theological feminists; there must be freedom even for "minorities." But since the ministry of pastors must be grounded in theological understanding of what we are doing, and since preaching requires intellectual clarity for its articulation, feminist and womanist theologies (for there are more than one of each) will have great impact on future generations of women pastors and through their ministry on the church. There has been a rude awakening in Christendom to the thousands of ways in which the church's venerable language habits and its thought patterns constitute not *the* theological universe, but that universe as perceived and articulated by men.

Thus one can expect a radical and deep renewal both of Faith and Order, and of Life and Work in the church as coming generations of women find language and structures that are truly theirs, as the male theologians and pastors have been doing for millennia claiming a false universality. A new language will be born, unless the church chooses to counsel its abortion.

With a critical mass—in both senses of "critical"—of women theologians given space and time in the life of our churches I anticipate a renewal and reformation of Christian perceptions— or rather of the language, thought structures and leadership models that express those perceptions. For women's perceptions have been there all the time, but hardly allowed to be heard and even less to be cultivated. I anticipate a new poetry and a new prose, perhaps in that order. I think of the various attempts at inclusive language as the mere scaffolding for that enterprise, barely begun. The ". . . or she" is a powerful sign for consciousness raising, but hardly the new poetry.

That theological enterprise will require that women pastors think of themselves as theologians, not just as applying a theology manufactured for them in their seminaries, not even by feminist teachers in seminaries. The model of ministers as practitioners, placed between the theoreticians in the schools and the consumers in the churches, that warmed-over model is doubly wrong for women pastors for whom there are yet too few givens. For them it is doubly true that each sermon is a an act of theological creativity, and each congregational meeting a search for the right process of accountability in Christ.

Since I will not live to see and be enriched by all that will happen in this renewal through the empowerment—to use a condescending word for a wonderful thing—of women, allow me to write down a few words about what has happened to me as I have been stimulated by feminist perspectives. As I have tried to listen to feminist deconstruction and reconstruction, few insights have meant more to me than the critique of adversarial/ binary thought habits, and their cousins, the hierarchies of people or of values. For example, if we are to lay bare the roots of violence in Christianity, Islam, and Judaism, what is more important than a deconstruction of the ultimately paranoid dichotomy of *we* and *they*? It then becomes important that *Shalom/Salam* does not mean peace by victory, but by harmony, the complex interplay where nothing is too big and nothing too small.

Adversative thinking permeates our theological traditions, especially in their Western form, where absolute distinctions order the universe, and our Barthian souls are horrified by the Eastern Orthodox insistence that the aim of the Christian life is divinization, that is, the restoration of the *imago dei*. The formative symbol system of Eastern Christianity is neither "God as judge—humans as sinners," nor "God as Lord—humans as slaves, servants, or citizens." The Eastern world is rather like the Johannine world where the symbols are organic, like the vine, the seed, and the water. It is all about life. Jesus came "that they may have life, and have it abundantly (John 10:10)." It was in listening to feminist theology that this whole world of a non-adversarial, organic symbol system, so much akin to the world of the life sciences, became a liberating alternative for my intellectual spirituality.

In that setting the critique of the overwhelming male imaging of God opened my eyes to how anthropomorphism, picturing God as a human person, has been allowed to reign unchecked. It may seem strange to many, but for me this led to a new appreciation of the Holy Trinity in the non-psychological and non-hierarchical organic understanding of the East. Not too long ago I put it this way:

KRISTER STENDAHL

But I begin to see that my faith badly needs to be challenged by the Trinity, by the mystery that rescues me from picturing God in all-too-human form. It could be argued that no earlier period of the church has pictured God more as a "human" Father and Jesus as a man than these last hundred years or so. Thereby the male image of God became oppressive to many women, and by implication also to men. What a liberation to be reminded that it is equally true to speak of God as Spirit—and in Greek the Spirit is *it*, not he or He! As the theology of the church was articulated and written by men, this non-gender character was lost by assimilation within the masculine God-language. Such an assimilation strikes many as inevitable, especially when the Latin term *persona*, with its original connotation of "role," became the translation of what the Greeks called *hypostasis* by which they expressed the concrete (substantive) manifestation of the one divine essence. But "person" spoke so much more directly to our need for a personal relation to God. And if the Spirit is a "person," then it seemed to require a personal pronoun.

In the church that turned out to be *he*, although in Hebrew the Spirit is *she*, as is her sister Wisdom in both Hebrew and Greek (*Sophia*).

I have come to experience the worship of the triune God as a liberation from that spiritual or intellectual idolatry in which we picture God in our own image. To be sure, we can pray to God in the most intimate personal terms. But when we are in danger of letting our images of God harden into idols with our own racial or gender traits, the image changes into the "non-image" for spirit, and those who worship God must worship in spirit and truth (John 4:24).

So we learn to image God beyond our imaging and imagining, a mystery that is not in the image of splendid isolation but eternal being in mutual inter-relationships, organic, cosmic life-giving energy, creative and transcendent.[3]

Those are some musings of an old male theologian and should be read as such. I offer them in gratitude for what some feminist perceptions have triggered in my mind. Women theologians—pastors and teachers—will no doubt see differently and different things, but I maintain the conviction that once they have space, time, and critical mass, they will reclaim classical traditions however tainted and skewed. Actually, the more visible, obvious, even obnoxious the male bias and the stereotyping appears in the texts and the systems, the better deconstruction can be followed up by reclaiming classical Christian traditions in a new key.[4]

The time may even come when one can read the sexist codes of the tradition as a Jewish lover of Shakespeare reads the antisemitic code of Shylock within its dramatic function. But that may take time, for the hurt is deep and the dangers of not laying bare the oppressive bias that exists in text and tradition is real. In ending on that note I have a special text in mind, one of the truly central passages in the gospels, a text that presupposes a typical stereotyping of the role and nature of women in order to make the point intended by the evangelist. As with Shylock, you have to accept the ruse, however offensive, to get the point. I am referring to the Gospel for Easter according to Mark (16:1-8), where the whole gospel ends on the note ". . . and [the women] went out and fled from the tomb, for terror and amazement had seized them; and they said nothing to anyone, for they were afraid."

Mark's whole gospel is permeated by the perception that the church lives in the "not yet." Peter and the disciples are scolded for any element of triumphalism. The cross, not the crown, is the sign of the times. In Mark—different from the other gospels and later additions to Mark— even the events of Easter morning are preliminary and anticipatory. They are non-events. To make that point abundantly clear Mark describes the event as taking place in the realm of women. As in so many cultures, women can move safely in the realm of death, caring for the corpse. They are told to tell the men, for women are not valid witnesses and they are so emotional and overly excited anyway, and easily scared so they didn't even tell. . . . So says Mark, to make sure nothing has *really* happened yet. It will, however, when it happens in Galilee—in the presence of the men—"the disciples and Peter." Here the very point of Mark's Gospel presupposes the negative stereotyping of women. However offensive, there it is. Unless one can read that code, the texts easily become tepid and banal.

As I offer this parting exercise in exegesis, I notice with great satisfaction that *The Women's Bible Commentary* breaks with the romantic interpretation of Luke as the primary source for a Christian theology of the role of women. On the contrary, it is Luke who stereotypes women as docile and submissive. The abrasive Canaanite mother of Matthew and Mark is not in Luke, nor John's Samaritan woman who answers back. It is Luke who shows us a devout Elizabeth and Anna to Matthew's Tamar, Rahab, Ruth, and Bathsheba as women in the ambience of the Birth Narratives.

This augurs well for the renewal also of biblical studies, the renewal which comes with new eyes. It makes me glad and confident, for I am a Lutheran who believes that "the word of God is not chained" (2 Timothy 2:9); certainly not chained to the andro-centricities and biases of the biblical authors or interpreters. I anticipate a renewal of vision and insight, a revival of biblical faith when women will give us the Word. It will be painful at times but another verse will glow with new intensity:

Indeed, the word of God is alive and active, sharper than any two-edged sword, piercing until it divides soul from spirit, joints from marrow; it is able to judge the thoughts and intentions of the heart (Hebrews 4:12).

Notes

1. It can hardly be a secret that much of my thinking has happened in conversation with Brita Stendahl. It was actually her father, the Rev. Joh. W. Johnsson who, as a member of Parliament, had moved that the question of women's ordination be taken up again (it had been raised a few times before). Brita Stendahl sharpened my eye for the dialectic between equality and complementarity. It is part of her analysis in *The Force of Tradition: A Case Study of Women Priests in Sweden*. The text includes an appendix by Constance F. Parvey, "Stir in the Ecumenical Movement: The Ordination of Women" (Fortress, 1985). That dialectic can be seen clearly in the life and writings of Sweden's first novelist and pioneering feminist Fredrika Bremer. Brita Stendahl's recent book about her demonstrates it more fully: *The Education of a Self-Taught Woman* (Edwin Mellen Press, 1994). It was also her *The Force of Tradition* that helped me see that there was more to "women's ordination" than I had thought. Hence the title of this article.

2. That is why the English translation of my contribution to the Swedish debate in the '50s has the subtitle *A Case Study in Hermeneutics*. It was published by Fortress Press in 1966 as *The Bible and the Role of Women*, and few copies were sold until the women's movement picked up momentum.

3. A quote from my *Energy for Life*, Reflections on the Theme of the 1991 WCC Assembly "Come Holy Spirit — Renew the Whole Creation" (Geneva: WCC 1990), pp. 6-7.

4. In her *Theology and Feminism* (Blackwell's, 1990), Daphne Hampson has argued powerfully that a Christian feminist theology is impossible if Christianity is to remain Christianity, and she has criticized those who "adjust" Christian texts and doctrines to make such a theology possible. Her stance is that of a post-Christian theologian. It is important to put equal emphasis on both *post* and *Christian*. It refers to a conscious and principled break with the Christian tradition, coupled with an equally conscious awareness that it is Christianity that one has broken with. In Daphne Hampson this is especially clear, and it makes her more free to appreciate the insights of the theological giants of the Christian tradition—all males, biased males. I remember

her saying that she of course had to take them seriously for, after all, they were the ones who had had the best opportunities for sustained and creative thought.

Perhaps the issue between Christian and post-Christian feminism centers in how one understands tradition — as a vehicle for stable continuity, or as a vehicle for organic development and growth of insight. If the latter, feminism can enrich and enliven Christianity. If the former, feminism is incompatible with Christianity. To me faithful interpretation is faith-filled interpretation and living tradition is organic change.

5. Carol A. Newsom and Sharon H. Ringe, editors, *The Women's Bible Commentary* (Louisville, KY: Westminster/John Knox Press, 1992). The Lukan commentary is by Jane Shaberg.

TRADITIONING,
TRUTH-TELLING,
TRANSFORMING

Karen L. Bloomquist

THE ARTICLES in this volume reflect some of the changes
Lutheran clergywomen have weathered during the past twenty-
five years, changes in how we view ourselves, the church, and
the ministries we are about. It was far easier to identify the com-
monalities of our struggles twenty years ago when our numbers
were less than one-hundredth of what they are today! To try to
generalize for all ordained Lutheran women today risks over-
looking our significantly different histories, experiences, and perceptions. It is not our uniformity but our real diversity of ages
and experiences, routes to ordination, call patterns since ordination, gifts for ministry, and contexts of our ministries that
have most enriched the ministry of the church.

I recall participating in the exuberance at the 1970 conventions of both the Lutheran Church in America (LCA) and the
American Lutheran Church (ALC), when the official decisions
were made to ordain women. Those of us who were among the
first female Master of Divinity students at Lutheran seminaries
were considered anomalies by both our professors and classmates. We were sought out as curiosities by local media and
other organizations in ways our male colleagues were not. Our
presence at clergy gatherings was awkward, because it disrupted
an all-male club. We did not fit into either the preconceived male
image of a pastor or into the ready-made clergy shirts.

To overcome the hurdles of getting in, much less making it through seminary, our sense of self-esteem and commitment had to be high; otherwise, we could not have survived. The support of other women was key; their reality checks helped assure us that we were not crazy. With them we experienced relief in not having to justify ourselves, an intuitive sense of what one another was saying, and a joy in naming and celebrating together the sustaining presence of a gracious God.

A decade later, we had become a small but noticeable ingredient in the mix of Lutheran pastors. Our numbers in seminaries were growing significantly. The influences we brought to seminary, our experiences in seminary, and how we viewed ourselves as women in ministry were becoming more diverse. I recall teaching a seminary class, recounting what it was like in the early 1970s, and hearing the response, "Oh, those were the dark ages!" Greater acceptance was assumed, at least until some jarring experiences during internship or first call.

Many of us yearned to be seen simply as pastors, without attention being focused on the modifier "woman." Some of us continued to welcome opportunities to gather together as women, sharing common concerns. Others stayed away from such gatherings, cautious about being associated with "feminist" agendas. Increasingly, we clergywomen were not all the same, nor were our issues the same. The differences among us still perplex people who want to generalize about "women pastors." There are more of us from which to choose, or to play off against one another. In the early years we celebrated the freedom we enjoyed because there was not yet an ideal image of a Lutheran clergywoman against which we could be measured. However, by now there are unspoken criteria by which some are considered more acceptable than others. Some of us are considered "good" and others "bad," according to the degree to which we go along with or challenge patriarchal assumptions and structures. "Divide and conquer" is not a new but a very old strategy by which women and other groups have been kept in their place.

Instead of allowing ourselves to be pitted against one another in either/or, win/lose dynamics of competition, a different vision is needed. I propose an intertwined spiral movement of traditioning, truth-telling, and transforming. Such a spiral metaphor does not imply unambiguous forward progress, which may be questionable theologically as well as empirically. Instead, the past and probably the next twenty-five years involve back-and-forth movement in which new implications of what it means to be faithful to God amid particular contexts and challenges are continually being discovered.

One of the major ways in which we are pitted against one another is in terms of our relation to Christian tradition. How feminist or how traditional we are is a key way in which distinctions are made about us. As clergywomen, our relation to Christian tradition cannot help but be somewhat ambivalent. On the one hand, the tradition of God acting in Jesus Christ has decisively shaped us. The liberating core of the gospel and the movement it impelled ground and empower us. Lutheran articulations of this freeing gospel are what have grasped or kept us connected with this particular expression of the church catholic. The gracious, compassionate God of justice revealed through Scripture is at the core of the faith we feel compelled to preach and live. But, on the other hand, many aspects of the tradition as passed on through Scripture and church history have helped perpetuate patriarchal domination and oppression of women and other marginalized groups. Our relation to tradition is an ongoing spiral, of saying "yes, but" and "even though." We are grounded in a faith tradition, see its underside and contradictions, but nevertheless continue to affirm it, albeit critically.

Our very presence as ordained ministers of Word and sacrament embodies this ambivalence: Who we are defies aspects of the historical tradition, but in that defiance, the liberating core of the tradition breaks through as we proclaim and enact God's presence. Each of us is, to varying degrees, the Syrophoenician or Canaanite woman who dared to talk back to Jesus (Mark 7:24-30; Matthew 15:21-28). She had to break the accepted rules of conduct in order to be heard; she intruded upon men's company and conversation; she dared to speak in public. Concern for the future, symbolized in the well-being of her daughter, impelled her to claim the right to confront Jesus. Because of her tenacious faith, she could not keep from challenging traditions that separate and exclude. She not only challenged but talked back to tradition. And in that talking back, that critiquing of tradition, she refused to be dismissed or caricatured. She embodies an authority not of privileged status but of determined purpose.

In recent years, as some of us began entering more visible positions of leadership in synods, seminaries, and other expressions of the church, it appeared that much was changing. Our presence in these structures has made a difference! However, we find ourselves standing on shifting ground that sometimes seems to be rumbling beneath our feet. Unresolved subliminal issues remain, which can contribute toward backlash. Overcoming the tradition of excluding women from ordained ministry was one hurdle, but a more difficult hurdle is the resistance to full acceptance of women as carriers, definers, and shapers of Christian tradition.

Even when we are ordained and have advanced theological degrees, we still are seen by some people not primarily as pastors or theologians of the church, but as *women* pastors and *women* theologians. The normative tradition of the church often still is set over and against what women are about. Certain feminist perspectives are dismissed as "ideological" and accused of being "corrosive . . . of the classical biblical and Christian tradition."[1] Whether or not we intentionally challenge the tradition, our very presence continues to be experienced by some as a threat to tradition.

We have entered some positions of influence but that does not mean our authority is always accepted. Male authorities are still turned to for the final word. "Inclusivity" is often juxtaposed to "competence." A committee, for example, is said to be lacking in theological expertise or parish clergy if the theologians and parish pastors on it are female rather than male. Women are assumed to be there primarily because of their gender. If they are also persons of color, they become even more suspect.

In our wider culture today, "traditional values" are being reasserted with a vengeance. Typically this involves a defense of the nuclear family. Traditional sex roles are advocated. The "traditional values" slogan points back to a time when "women knew their place." That served as a linchpin for a stable social order. From this perspective, women in non-traditional roles such as the ordained ministry inevitably are seen as threats to such an order.

More than once I have received phone calls from persons with disgruntled church members who at some point in the conversation have traced their complaints over "what's wrong with the church today" back to the decision to ordain women. When I now hear staunch calls in the Evangelical Lutheran Church in America (ELCA) to "defend" or "get back to the tradition," I increasingly wonder what about the tradition needs to be defended? To what do we need to "go back"? Has "the tradition" in such polemics become a new code word for a yearning to return to a time before women were ordained in the Lutheran church? Is the call for a return to "tradition" similar to the early church's household codes in the Pastoral Epistles, which had the effect of putting women back in their place?

Part of our calling as clergywomen today is to remind the church that the faith tradition that shapes and guides us is not a static noun but a dynamic verb of *traditioning*. A static tradition can become an idolatrous means of oppression. In contrast, traditioning "witnesses to the presence of God in Jesus Christ and in our lives, but its meaning changes as the context of the message and the messengers changes. . . . Human beings are continually traditioning a body of past knowledge." This traditioning makes it possible for us to move into the future. It is "the still living, evolving past by which we create the future."[2] The new perspectives, insights, and ways of being church that women bring can potentially help to renew the whole church.

Traditioning is to be expected in a church that is continually being reformed through the power of God's dynamic Word. The Lutheran Confessions were key in calling the church back to the animating Word of God in all its particularities. Insisting on strict allegiance to certain understandings of the Bible or the Confessions without a lively sense of their reforming implications for us today can become a means of control or manipulation. It is not abstract formulas but the dynamic, creating, redeeming, renewing activity of God to which they bear witness that is at stake.

Proclamation of this transforming Word and celebration of the sacraments become means of resistance to ways of thinking and acting that control, dominate, and seek to manage what is different or "other." The Bible speaks truth through its address of specific social issues and of the relationships, orders, and rules that create and perpetuate those situations.

Proclamation is a truth-telling that leads to reordering, heralding, and reforming. Proclamation sets free an anticipatory freedom.[3] For us as clergywomen to speak this truth of God is to risk touching deep anxieties, or even becoming targets of reactionary attacks. Yet we cannot keep quiet when people and institutions abuse and exploit.

It is also risky but important to engage in truth-telling with one another as women in ministry. We do not all agree and are not united just because we are female. We differ significantly in our experiences, perspectives, and relative power. Not only do others use these differences to separate us, but we can and do use them against one another. Critique of one another is difficult but a sign of maturity. Our value is not maintained by denying the value of those who are different from ourselves, whether they be female or male. We need to talk truthfully about how we as women threaten and are threatened by one another. Tendencies to inflate our own perceptions and judgments, using them to generalize for all women, must be challenged. We who are white women need especially to hear these challenges from women of color. We need the challenging perspective of those who are other from us in order to keep us from taking our partial perspectives too seriously. Closing ourselves off from critique becomes a way of losing the truth that sets free.

Through truth-telling, transformation occurs. As a gathered assembly of Word and sacrament, the church lives through nurturing and celebrating values of "difference, specificity, embodiment, solidarity, anticipation, and transformation."[4] Transformation entails discovery, surprise, nuance, insight, judgment, interrogation, and struggle. This is much of what the past twenty-five years have been like. Through it all, the church *has* been transformed. Most of this transformation has occurred in local settings, in subtle, quiet ways as women have tenaciously carried out their ministries. Truth-telling has occurred, lives have been transformed, and new traditioning has occurred.

After twenty-five years, clergywomen definitely are "in" the Evangelical Lutheran Church in America. We are making significant differences in its life, and in numbers few anticipated in 1970. But there still are ways in which we are not yet "of" the institutional church. As of spring 1995, only one woman was serving as executive director of a churchwide division, none as a seminary president or academic dean, and only two as synodical bishops.[5] The strategic decisions and directions of the church are still mostly determined by white clergymen. These things too must change.

In the meantime, being "in" but not yet "of" the institution is not necessarily a bad place to be. When we truly do become "of" the institution, then we risk losing the critical, liberating, transforming dynamic of the faith that our age-old marginality has helped us discern and appreciate. May we today and in the future join the prophet Miriam and "all the women" (Exodus 15:20-21), dancing a spiral of traditioning, truth-telling, and transforming, and singing in praise of all that God has done and will continue to do. Amen.

Notes

1. Robert Benne, *The Paradoxical Vision: A Public Theology for the Twenty-first Century* (Minneapolis: Fortress, 1995), pp. 53-54.
2. Letty M. Russell, *Church in the Round: Feminist Interpretations of the Church* (Louisville, Ky.: Westminster, 1993), p. 38.
3. Rebecca S. Chopp, *The Power to Speak: Feminism, Language, God* (Boston: Crossroad, 1989), pp. 59.
4. *Ibid.*, p. 76.
5. On June 2, 1995, Andrea F. DeGroot-Nesdahl was elected bishop of the South Dakota Synod, Evangelical Luthern Church in America.

CONTRIBUTORS

Margaret Barth Wold is primarily a communicator who has spoken to thousands of groups on a variety of subjects and has written numerous books, articles, and studies. Seemingly destined to be a pioneer, she was appointed to an *ad hoc* committee whose task it was to study and recommend the ordination of women to the ALC. She has served as Executive Director of American Lutheran Church Women, as Director for Ministry in Changing Communities for the ALC, and as a professor of religion at California Lutheran University. She was the first woman in thirty-five years to be selected to give the Hein Memorial Lectures at the four seminaries of the ALC in 1985.

Dorothy J. Marple was increasingly influential in bringing Lutheran women into the whole life of the LCA and the church worldwide. She served as Executive Director of Lutheran Church Women from 1962 to 1975. Subsequently she served as assistant to President Robert J. Marshall and Bishop James R. Crumley, Jr., and as coordinator for the Commission for a New Lutheran Church (CNLC), the transition team charged with bringing the ELCA into being. Currently she is chairperson of the Evangelical Lutheran Church in America (ELCA) Task Force on the Study of Theological Education for Ministry.

Mary Todd is completing her Ph.D. in history with a concentration in women's studies at the University of Illinois at Chicago. Her dissertation addresses the question of the ordination of women in The Lutheran Church–Missouri Synod.

Gracia Grindal is a professor of rhetoric at Luther Seminary, St. Paul, Minnesota. A poet and hymnwriter, she is also a student of history, especially as it has to do with women in Scandinavian and Scandinavian Lutheran contexts.

Elizabeth Platz serves as campus pastor at the University of Maryland at College Park. She enjoys serving on a number of university committees and being a part of the committees and work of the synod. She was recently named Outstanding Woman of the Year at the University of Maryland and distinguished alumna by The Lutheran Theological Seminary at Gettysburg.

Susan Thompson and Barbara Andrews were friends from 1972 until Andrew's death in 1978. Thompson served from 1974 through 1987 as the ALC Service Mission Director to Wisconsin and was an editor of the ALC newsletter, "Women and Men Becoming." She presently is program director for newly organized congregations in the ELCA Division for Outreach and lives in Park Ridge, Illinois.

Janith Maureen Otte is a psychotherapist in private practice, working primarily with survivors of child abuse and persons dealing with life transitions and eating disorders. She lives in Oakland, California.

Stephanie K. Frey was ordained in July of 1982. She served as an associate pastor at Christ the King Lutheran Church, Mankato, Minnesota, from 1982-1986 and as co-pastor of First Lutheran Church, St. James, Minnesota from 1986-1993. After being awarded a Leadership Fellowship from the Bush Foundation of Minnesota in 1993, Frey took a study leave to attend Duke Divinity School, Durham, North Carolina, where she completed a Th.M. in homiletics and church history in December, 1994. She currently serves as synod minister on the staff of the Southwestern Minnesota Synod, ELCA, Redwood Falls Minnesota.

Norma Cook Everist is Professor of Church and Ministry at Wartburg Theological Seminary, Dubuque, Iowa, where she has served since 1979. From 1976 to 1979 she taught at Yale Divinity School in New Haven, Connecticut. She was consecrated a Lutheran deaconess in 1960. She has served parishes in St. Louis, Missouri and in New Haven and Hamden, Connecticut.

Margaret Herz-Lane was born and raised on the south side of Chicago. She attended Luther College in Decorah, Iowa, graduating in 1969 with a B.A. in art and French. She worked for Augustana Academy (Canton, South Dakota), Luther College, (Decorah, Iowa) and Luther College of the Bible and Liberal Arts (Teaneck, New Jersey) between 1969 and 1977. She attended Luther Northwestern Theological Seminary, graduating in 1981, and has served as a pastor of the Camden Lutheran Parish, Camden, New Jersey, since then.

Barbara J. Lundblad was ordained in the LCA in 1980. She currently serves as pastor of Our Saviour's Atonement Lutheran Church in New York City. Lundblad is regularly asked to preach or to address the subject of preaching at conferences and institutes. In 1987 she was the preacher for the opening worship at the ELCA Constituting Convention. She has served as adjunct faculty in homiletics at Yale Divinity School, Union Theological Seminary, and Princeton Theological Seminary.

Mary E. F. Albing is a parish pastor serving St. Peder's Lutheran Church in Minneapolis, Minnesota. During her husband's pastoral internship year in Madagascar, she was instrumental in starting a health clinic serving Malagasy seminarians and their families. She has written numerous Bible studies, curricula, and worship materials. A busy public speaker, she has been featured at numerous women's events. She has also preached and led congregational renewal and leadership growth retreats and long-range planning events for a variety of organizations. She has served as pastor of Trinity Parish in Hannaford, North Dakota and United Lutheran in Grand Forks, North Dakota. In addition she and her husband have served as interim ministers in nine congregations in North Dakota and Minnesota.

Carolyn Mercedes Mowchan is a graduate of Gustavus Adolphus College and Luther Northwestern Theological Seminary. She and her husband serve Trinity Lutheran Church in Spooner, Wisconsin. Areas of interest beyond ministry are: writing for publication, teaching piano, teaching liturgical dance, and spending time outdoors.

Cynthia Ganzkow-Wold, ordained in 1977, is currently serving as senior pastor of St. Luke's, Middleton, Wisconsin where she oversees a large congregation and a multiple staff. She earned degrees from the University of Minnesota and Luther Seminary. She has served as campus pastor at the University of Wisconsin, Madison, as associate pastor at Bethlehem Lutheran, Aberdeen, South Dakota and as co-pastor at Bison Lutheran, Bison, South Dakota. She was the first female pastor assigned to parish ministry in South Dakota in 1977.

Margaret A. Krych was an ordained Methodist minister in Australia before coming to the U.S. in 1970 to do Ph.D. studies at Princeton Theological Seminary. She was ordained in the LCA in 1973. She served on Lutheran Church in America (LCA) churchwide staff from 1973 to 1977 as editor of early elementary resources for the Division for Parish Services. In May of 1977 she took a call to Lutheran Theological Seminary at Philadelphia where she currently is the Charles Norton Professor of Christian Education and Theology.

Cheryl Stewart Pero is the president of the African American Lutheran Association. She coordinates Crossings Ministry, a ministry that brings together the resources of Lutheran Campus Ministry of Metropolitan Chicago, Lutheran Social Services of Illinois, the Chicago City Colleges, and the African American congregations in the South Conference of the Metropolitan Chicago Synod of the ELCA.

April Ulring Larson was elected bishop of the La Crosse Area Synod on June 12, 1992. Her election made her the first Lutheran woman bishop in the Western Hemisphere and second in the world. Larson did her undergraduate work at Luther College and the University of Iowa. She later attended Wartburg Seminary and graduated with a Master of Divinity in December 1977. She served three successive parishes in Iowa before becoming an assistant to the bishop in the Southeastern Minnesota Synod and while serving there, was elected bishop of the La Crosse Area Synod.

Mary Ann Moller-Gunderson is a native of the Northwest. She received her Master of Divinity degree from Lutheran School of Theology at Chicago in 1977, and served parishes in Portland, Oregon, Stevenson, Washington, and Madison, Wisconsin. Moller-Gunderson accepted a call as assistant to the bishop of the Greater Milwaukee Synod in 1988. While serving on synod staff she became extensively involved in staffing matters of clergy sexual abuse. In 1992 she left her synod position to become executive director of the ELCA Division for Congregational Ministries. She left that post in April 1995 to serve as pastor of Immanuel Lutheran Church in Lake Geneva, Wisconsin.

Phyllis Anderson currently serves as Director for Theological Education in the Division for Ministry of the ELCA. Ordained in 1978, Anderson served the Tri-Lutheran Parish in Dyersville, Epworth, and Earlville, Iowa from 1979-1983. Subsequently she was assistant to the bishop of the Iowa District, ALC and Director for Pastoral Studies on the faculty of the Lutheran School of Theology at Chicago. She holds a Master of Divinity degree from Wartburg Theological Seminary, a Ph.D. in theology from Aquinas Institute of Theology, and an honorary doctorate from Susquehanna University.

Krister Stendahl is Andrew W. Mellon Professor of Divinity Emeritus at Harvard University and Bishop Emeritus of Stockholm, Sweden. His writings center in biblical studies, from which perspective he has addressed various issues of theology, history, the arts of ministry, and contemporary problems in church and society. Since the early 1950s he has written on the role of women in the Bible. Asked why women became such a focus for his biblical and theological work, he answered: "The Christian Bible includes sayings that have caused pain to . . . women. Thus I have felt called to seek forms of interpretation which can counteract such undesirable side effect of the Holy Scriptures."

Karen L. Bloomquist was ordained in the ALC in 1974 and became the first Lutheran woman called to pastor a congregation in the western part of the U.S. She has been a pastor of congregations in Oakland, California and Brooklyn, N.Y. She received her Ph. D. in theology from Union Theological Seminary in New York City. In 1982 she began teaching at Lutheran School of Theology at Chicago, and since 1988 has been Director for Studies in the ELCA Division for Church in Society.